THE WIDOWING OF MRS HOLROYD

AND

THE DAUGHTER-IN-LAW

These two plays, set in the Nottinghamshire mining area Lawrence knew so well, make a good introduction to Lawrence's less well known skill as a playwright. He wanted to give a voice to the working people he knew and to make it truly their voice.

THE HEREFORD PLAYS

General Editor: E. R. Wood

***

Peter Barnes
The Ruling Class

Robert Bolt
A Man for All Seasons

Harold Brighouse
Hobson's Choice

Chapman and Coxe
Billy Budd

Nikolai Gogol
The Government Inspector

Greenwood and Gow
Love on the Dole

Willis Hall
The Long and the Short and the Tall

Stanley Houghton
Hindle Wakes

Henrik Ibsen
An Enemy of the People

D. H. Lawrence
The Widowing of Mrs Holroyd and The Daughter-in-Law

Arthur Miller
The Crucible
Death of a Salesman
All My Sons
A View From the Bridge

Bill Naughton
Spring and Port Wine

André Obey
Noah

Clifford Odets
Golden Boy

John Patrick
The Teahouse of the August Moon

Luigi Pirandello
Six Characters in Search of an Author

J. B. Priestley
An Inspector Calls
When We Are Married

James Saunders
Next Time I'll Sing to You

R. C. Sherriff
Journey's End

David Storey
In Celebration

J. M. Synge
The Playboy of the Western World and *Riders to the Sea*

Brandon Thomas
Charley's Aunt

Peter Ustinov
Romanoff and Juliet

John Whiting
A Penny for a Song

Oscar Wilde
The Importance of Being Earnest

Emlyn Williams
The Corn is Green
Night Must Fall

Tennessee Williams
The Glass Menagerie

D. H. Lawrence

The Widowing of Mrs Holroyd
&
The Daughter-in-Law

with an Introduction by
RAY SPEAKMAN

HEINEMANN
EDUCATIONAL

Heinemann Educational Books Ltd
Halley Court, Jordan Hill, Oxford OX2 8EJ

OXFORD LONDON EDINBURGH
MADRID ATHENS BOLOGNA PARIS
MELBOURNE SYDNEY AUCKLAND
IBADAN NAIROBI HARARE GABORONE
SINGAPORE TOKYO PORTSMOUTH NH (USA)

ISBN 0 435 22569 3

91 92 93 94 95 11 10 9 8 7 6 5 4 3 2

Printed in England by Clays Ltd, St Ives plc

Contents

AN INTRODUCTION FOR THE STUDENT

1 Reading the plays

Plays are meant to be acted. If they cannot be acted then at the very least they are meant to be read out loud, not silently and privately. This is true of all plays. With these two plays by D. H. Lawrence it is not only important that they be read out loud, it is vital. Lawrence was interested in the way people spoke, the words they used, the way they shaped language in their own individual ways, how the way they spoke revealed what they were, and particularly, the way they could use everyday, ordinary speech in rhythms which were almost poetic. Lawrence thought that many of the writers of his time were not interested in the way people spoke—at least not the people Lawrence wanted to write about. He wanted to put working class people into plays: the 'submerged' class he called them. They were submerged because they did not have a voice, particularly in the theatre.

If you are to enjoy these plays, and understand them, and be true to what Lawrence wanted, then you must take into consideration his intention to realistically and accurately reproduce the language of those people he was writing about. This will make reading what he has written difficult *unless* you prepare beforehand. Once you have mastered the sometimes difficult language patterns (and it really does only take a short time to get used to the contractions and vocabulary) you will not also be helping the rest of your group understand and enjoy the plays, but you will also be doing justice to Lawrence and the people he was so eager to give a voice to.

In *The Daughter-in-Law* all the characters, except for Minnie, speak with a heavy local accent and dialect. In *The Widowing of Mrs Holroyd*, only Charles Holroyd and his mother speak in this way. Most of the parts in both plays are long, so careful preparation is essential.

2 After reading the plays

There are suggestions for follow-up activities at the end of this book. They fall under four headings: 'Keeping Track', 'Explorations', 'Special Studies' and 'Looking at the two plays together'.

'Keeping Track' consists of detailed questions about the text. These are intended to encourage a close reading of the plays and might be used for writing, discussion or as a guide for a 'reading journal'. Apart from helping you to discover if you have understood what you have heard and read, they are also intended to point you towards some of Lawrence's main concerns.

'Explorations' invites you to apply your imagination to the plays and at the same time to look again at the texts in detail. The suggestions here might prove useful for medium length coursework pieces.

'Special Studies' are suggestions for coursework pieces of considerable length. 'Looking at the two plays together' similarly invites you to consider the plays in extended pieces of writing. Both these sections contain suggestions for a wider reading of Lawrence's work.

Ray Speakman 1988

GLOSSARY

Speech contractions

In order to reproduce as exactly as possible the speech of the Nottinghamshire mining community, Lawrence uses the apostrophe for omission frequently. It is impossible to list every example of this, but the following list should help you understand Lawrence's approach.

a'	all (double l is often omitted—as in Watna' for Watnall)
arena	aren't
bu'r	but a
'em	them
ha'in	having
I s'd ha'	I should have
I s'll	I shall
isna	isn't
i'th'	in the
ma'e	make
sin'	since
tha'lt	thou will
the'	there
'ud	would
wi'	with
worna	weren't
wouldna	wouldn't

Dialect and mining words

addle: earn

after-damp: carbon dioxide which rises after an explosion of fire-damp (a combustible gas, usually methane) in a coal mine. *After-damp* suffocates.

a-gait: going on, happening.

all of a work: in a state of fermentation.

American cutters: a form of mechanical coal cutter (See *Iron-men* below)

anigh: nigh or near

'appen: perhaps ('happen')

a-whoam: at home

ax: ask

bantle: the group of men who ride in the pit cage at any one time. (As a safety precaution there is a maximum number allowed.)

baulkin': thwarting, hindering

bitted an' bobbed: tricked and cheated, trifled with

blort, blortin': to bellow loudly

bobbled: hurried away, disappeared

bobby: impertinent

brake: horse drawn vehicle

bully-raggin': to annoy someone by irritating language

butties: works alongside of

butty: generally a comrade or work-fellow, but here used more precisely of a man who takes a contract for the work of a group.

'casions: occasion

chalked of a line: thoroughly reproved. The local saying is: 'I gave her a good chalking off.'

chunterin': muttering and grumbling

clat-fart: to gossip (*clat* is idle tales)

claver: idle talk

club-money: a weekly payment that can be drawn from the *club* during sickness or unemployment if regular payments have been put in

clunch: a hard clay material

coddled: pampered and fussed over

come-day-go-day: a ditherer

cratch: the rack or crib used to hold hay in a stable or cow shed; hence 'feed', and presumably here means: 'never on time for the meal'.

day man: a miner who worked for a daily rate of pay given by the *butty* (see above) who contracted with the mining company. The *day man* was thus less well off and had less status than the *butty*.

dog's nose: a mixture of whiskey and beers

doited: crazy or childish

enow: enough

flig: fully-fledged and able to fly; Mr Purdy means, presumably that an inexperienced person would have spoken

foisty: musty and stale

fow: foul, and therefore disagreeable or offensive

fudge: to botch up

gaby: the foreman of a group of workers

gen/gie: give

gnaw: gnaw or chew

guyney: 'my guyney'—my word

hawksed: removed violently (i.e. 'I didn't have gas—he hawksed it out.' Speaking of a dentist's removal of a tooth)

headstocks: the winding gear at the head of the mine shaft

holin' a stint: to hole is a mining term meaning to cut a passageway or cut round a block of coal

injun: engine

iron-men: a coal-cutting machine used to undercut the coal, which could then be hewed out by hand more easily

jackin' up: to ruin

lief: *as lief*—rather

linking: looking

mard: to pamper or spoil

maun: must

more mark than mar: *mar* means injure or damage, and the phrase therefore means: 'it looks worse than it really is'

mort: a great amount

mosh: much or mash, something in a soft pulpy condition

natty: spruce and neat

neither one road nor t'other: neither one way or the other

orts and slarts: scraps left over from a meal

panchion: a large dish or bowl made of earthenware

pick-heft: pick handle

roads: the tunnels leading to the *stalls*. It was essential that the roads were kept clear, but although the job was less laborious than hewing at the face, it was hard and unrewarding, and regarded as menial unskilled work

rowdy: a form of *rody*—to describe bacon which is streaked with alternative layers of fat and lean

sawney: weak simpleton

scraightin': crying

scrawdrags: strike-breakers

selvidge: border of a sheet

shifting shirt: a change of shirt (*shifting* refers especially to a change of clothes for after working hours)

shiftly: probably the same as *shifty*, in the sense of ingenious or clever

shine: a display

sin': since; hence *A wik sin' today* is 'a week ago today'

slaver: spittle in the mouth, and therefore used for 'nonsense' or 'drivel'

slivin': slip secretly

slormed, slorm: to slink away, to go about with a hang-dog air (related to slumbering or dozing)

sluther: to slide or slip

slutherers: people who work hastily or carelessly

snaggin': biting (especially when suggesting nagging and scolding) *snap*: the miner's food, particularly the bread taken down the pit for the mid-day break

sotten: dialect form of 'sat'

stall: the section of the coal-face worked by one or two men on their own

stint: the day's task

stool-arsed Jack: office worker

strap: credit or 'tick'

swarf: dirty

tabs: ears

tacket: this may be just a rhyming word for the reduplication of the phrase 'racket and—', but in some parts of Northern England the word is used for the kind of nails used in hob-nailed-boots and even for a restless unruly boy

ter: you or, sometimes, to

throng: busy, crowded

thysen: yourself

tip-callin': gossip and slander

wallit: a left-handed person, hence clumsy here

Watna': Watnall

weritted: worried

wezzel-brained: weasel-brained

whoam: home

widders': widows'. Free coal had been allowed to the widows of miners

winden: a heavy blow

winders: windows

wringer: a type of crowbar used for prizing coal off the coal face

yi: yes

The Widowing of Mrs Holroyd

CHARACTERS

MRS HOLROYD

HOLROYD

BLACKMORE

JACK HOLROYD

MINNIE HOLROYD

GRANDMOTHER

RIGLEY

CLARA

LAURA

MANAGER

TWO MINERS

The action of the play takes place in the Holroyds' cottage

ACT ONE

SCENE ONE

The kitchen of a miner's small cottage. On the left is the fireplace, with a deep, full red fire. At the back is a white-curtained window, and beside it the outer door of the room. On the right, two white wooden stairs intrude into the kitchen below the closed stair-foot door. On the left, another door.

The room is furnished with a chintz-backed sofa under the window, a glass-knobbed painted dresser on the right, and in the centre, toward the fire, a table with a red and blue check tablecloth. On one side of the hearth is a wooden rocking-chair, on the other an arm-chair of round staves. An unlighted copper-shaded lamp hangs from the raftered ceiling. It is dark twilight, with the room full of warm fireglow. A woman enters from the outer door. As she leaves the door open behind her, the colliery rail can be seen not far from the threshold, and, away back, the headstocks of a pit.

The woman is tall and voluptuously built. She carries a basket heaped full of washing, which she has just taken from the clotheslines outside. Setting down the basket heavily, she feels among the clothes. She lifts out a white heap of sheets and other linen, setting it on the table; then she takes a woollen shirt in her hand.

MRS HOLROYD (*aloud, to herself*): You know they're not dry even now, though it's been as fine as it has. (*She spreads the shirt on the back of her rocking-chair, which she turns to the fire.*)

VOICE (*calling from outside*): Well, have you got them dry?

MRS HOLROYD *starts up, turns and flings her hand in the*

*direction of the open door, where appears a man in blue overalls,
swarfed and greased. He carries a dinner-basket.*

MRS HOLROYD: You—you—I don't know what to call you!
The idea of shouting at me like that—like the Evil One out
of the darkness!

BLACKMORE: I ought to have remembered your tender
nerves. Shall I come in?

MRS HOLROYD: No—not for your impudence. But you're
late, aren't you?

BLACKMORE: It's only just gone six. We electricians, you
know, we're the gentlemen on a mine: ours is gentlemen's
work. But I'll bet Charles Holroyd was home before four.

MRS HOLROYD (*bitterly*): Ay, and gone again before five.

BLACKMORE: But mine's a lad's job, and I do nothing!—
Where's he gone?

MRS HOLROYD (*contemptuously*): Dunno! He'd got a game
on somewhere—toffed himself up to the nines, and skedaddled off as brisk as a turkey-cock. (*She smirks in front of
the mirror hanging on the chimney-piece, in imitation of a man
brushing his hair and moustache and admiring himself.*)

BLACKMORE: Though turkey-cocks aren't brisk as a rule.
Children playing?

MRS HOLROYD (*recovering herself coldly*): Yes. And they ought
to be in.

*She continues placing the flannel garments before the fire, on
the fender and on chair-backs, till the stove is hedged in with a
steaming fence; then she takes a sheet in a bundle from the table,
and goes up to BLACKMORE, who stands watching her.*

Here, take hold, and help me fold it.

BLACKMORE: I shall swarf it up.

MRS HOLROYD (*snatching back the sheet*): Oh, you're as tire-
some as everybody else.

BLACKMORE (*putting down his basket and moving to door on
right*): Well, I can soon wash my hands.

MRS HOLROYD (*ceasing to flap and fold pillow-cases*): That

roller-towel's ever so dirty. I'll get you another. (*She goes to a drawer in the dresser, and then back toward the scullery, from which comes the sound of water.*)

BLACKMORE: Why, bless my life, I'm a lot dirtier than the towel. I don't want another.

MRS HOLROYD (*going into the scullery*): Here you are.

BLACKMORE (*softly, now she is near him*): Why did you trouble now? Pride, you know, pride, nothing else.

MRS HOLROYD (*also playful*): It's nothing but decency.

BLACKMORE (*softly*): Pride, pride, pride!

A child of eight suddenly appears in the doorway.

JACK: Oo, how dark!

MRS HOLROYD (*hurrying agitated into the kitchen*): Why, where have you been—what have you been doing now?

JACK (*surprised*): Why—I've only been out to play.

MRS HOLROYD (*still sharply*): And where's Minnie?

A little girl of six appears by the door.

MINNIE: I'm here, mam, and what do you think——?

MRS HOLROYD (*softening, as she recovers equanimity*): Well, and what should I think?

JACK: Oh, yes, mam—you know my father——?

MRS HOLROYD (*ironically*): I should hope so.

MINNIE: We saw him dancing, mam, with a paper bonnet.

MRS HOLROYD: What——?

JACK: There's some women at New Inn, what's come from Nottingham——

MINNIE: An' he's dancin' with the pink one.

JACK: Shut up, our Minnie. An' they've got paper bonnets on——

MINNIE: All colours, mam!

JACK (*getting angry*): Shut up, our Minnie! An' my dad's dancing with her.

MINNIE: With the pink-bonnet one, mam.

JACK: Up in the club-room over the bar.

MINNIE: An' she's a lot littler than him, mam.

JACK (*piteously*): Shut up, our Minnie—An' you can see 'em' go past the window, 'cause there isn't no curtains up, an my father's got the pink bonnet one——

MINNIE: An' there's a piano, mam—

JACK: An' lots of folk outside watchin', lookin' at my dad! He can dance, can't he, mam?

MRS HOLROYD (*she has been lighting the lamp, and holds the lamp-glass*): And who else is there?

MINNIE: Some more men—an' *all* the women with paper bonnets on.

JACK: There's about ten, I should think, an' they say they came in a brake from Nottingham.

MRS HOLROYD, *trying to replace the lamp-glass over the flame, lets it drop on the floor with a smash.*

JACK: There, now—now we'll have to have a candle.

BLACKMORE (*appearing in the scullery doorway with the towel*): What's that—the lamp-glass?

JACK: I never knowed Mr Blackmore was here.

BLACKMORE (*to* MRS HOLROYD): Have you got another?

MRS HOLROYD: No. (*There is silence for a moment.*) We can manage with a candle for to-night.

BLACKMORE (*stepping forward and blowing out the smoky flame*): I'll see if I can't get you one from the pit. I shan't be a minute.

MRS HOLROYD: Don't—don't bother—I don't want you to. *He, however, unscrews the burner and goes.*

MINNIE: Did Mr Blackmore come for tea mam?

MRS HOLROYD: No; he's had no tea.

JACK: I bet he's hungry. Can I have some bread?

MRS HOLROYD (*she stands a lighted candle on the table*): Yes, and you can get your boots off to go to bed.

JACK: It's not seven o'clock yet.

MRS HOLROYD: It doesn't matter.

MINNIE: What do they wear paper bonnets for, mam?

MRS HOLROYD: Because they're brazen hussies.

JACK: I saw them having a glass of beer.

MRS HOLROYD: A nice crew!

JACK: They say they are old pals of Mrs Meakins. You could hear her screaming o' laughin', an' my dad says: 'He-ah, missis—here—a dog's-nose for the Dachess—hopin' it'll smell samthing'—What's a dog's-nose?

MRS HOLROYD (*giving him a piece of bread and butter*): Don't ask me, child. How should I know?

MINNIE: Would she eat it, mam?

MRS HOLROYD: Eat what?

MINNIE: Her in the pink bonnet—eat the dog's-nose?

MRS HOLROYD: No, of course not. How should I know what a dog's-nose is?

JACK: I bet he'll never go to work to-morrow, mother—will he?

MRS HOLROYD: Goodness knows. I'm sick of it—disgracing me. There'll be the whole place cackling *this* now. They've no sooner finished about him getting taken up for fighting than they begin on this. But I'll put a stop to it some road or other. It's not going on, if I know it: it isn't.

She stops, hearing footsteps, and BLACKMORE *enters.*

BLACKMORE: Here we are then—got one all right.

MINNIE: Did they give it you, Mr Blackmore?

BLACKMORE: No, I took it.

He screws on the burner and proceeds to light the lamp. He is a tall, slender, mobile man of twenty-seven, brown-haired, dressed in blue overalls. JACK HOLROYD *is a big, dark, ruddy, lusty lad.* MINNIE *is also big, but fair.*

MINNIE: What do you wear blue trousers for, Mr Blackmore?

BLACKMORE: They're to keep my other trousers from getting greasy.

MINNIE: Why don't you wear pit-breeches, like dad's?

JACK: 'Cause he's a 'lectrician. Could you make me a little injun what would make electric light?

BLACKMORE: I will, some day.

JACK: When?

MINNIE: Why don't you come an' live here?

BLACKMORE (*looking swiftly at* MRS HOLROYD): Nay, you've got your own dad to live here.

MINNIE (*plaintively*): Well, you could come as well. Dad shouts when we've gone to bed, an' thumps the table. He wouldn't if you was here.

JACK: He dursn't——

MRS HOLROYD: Be quiet now, be quiet. Here, Mr Blackmore. (*She again gives him the sheet to fold.*)

BLACKMORE: Your hands *are* cold.

MRS HOLROYD: Are they?—I didn't know.

BLACKMORE *puts his hand on hers.*

MRS HOLROYD (*confusedly, looking aside*): You must want your tea.

BLACKMORE: I'm in no hurry.

MRS HOLROYD: Selvidge to selvidge. You'll be quite a domestic man, if you go on.

BLACKMORE: Ay.

They fold the two sheets.

BLACKMORE: They are white, your sheets!

MRS HOLROYD: But look at the smuts on them—look! This vile hole! I'd never have come to live here, in all the thick of the pit-grime, and lonely, if it hadn't been for him, so that he shouldn't call in a public-house on his road home from work. And now he slinks past on the other side of the railway, and goes down to the New Inn instead of coming in for his dinner. I might as well have stopped in Bestwood.

BLACKMORE: Though I rather like this little place, standing by itself.

MRS HOLROYD: Jack, can you go and take the stockings in for me? They're on the line just below the pigsty. The prop's near the apple-tree—mind it. Minnie, you take the peg-basket.

MINNIE: Will there be any rats, mam?

MRS HOLROYD: Rats—no. They'll be frightened when they hear you, if there are.

The children go out.

BLACKMORE: Poor little beggars!

MRS HOLROYD: Do you know, this place is fairly alive with rats. They run up that dirty vine in front of the house— I'm always at him to cut it down—and you can hear them at night overhead like a regiment of soldiers tramping. Really, you know, I *hate* them.

BLACKMORE: Well—a rat is a nasty thing!

MRS HOLROYD: But I s'll get used to them. I'd give anything to be out of this place.

BLACKMORE: It *is* rotten, when you're tied to a life you don't like. But I should miss it if you weren't here. When I'm coming down the line to the pit in the morning—it's nearly dark at seven now—I watch the firelight in here. Sometimes I put my hand on the wall outside where the chimney runs up to feel it warm. There isn't much in Bestwood, is there?

MRS HOLROYD: There's less than nothing if you can't be like the rest of them—as common as they're made.

BLACKMORE: It's a fact—particularly for a woman—But this place is cosy—God love me, I'm sick of lodgings.

MRS HOLROYD: You'll have to get married—I'm sure there are plenty of nice girls about.

BLACKMORE: Are there? I never see 'em. (*He laughs.*)

MRS HOLROYD: Oh, come, you can't say that.

BLACKMORE: I've not seen a single girl—an unmarried girl— that I should want for more than a fortnight—not one.

MRS HOLROYD: Perhaps you're very particular.

She puts her two palms on the table and leans back. He draws near to her, dropping his head.

BLACKMORE: Look here!

He has put his hand on the table near hers.

MRS HOLROYD: Yes, I know you've got nice hands—but you needn't be vain of them.

BLACKMORE: No—it's not that—But don't they seem—(*he glances swiftly at her; she turns her head aside; he laughs nervously*)—they sort of go well with one another. (*He laughs again.*)

MRS HOLROYD: They *do*, rather——

They stand still, near one another, with bent heads, for a moment. Suddenly she starts up and draws her hand away.

BLACKMORE: Why—what is it?

*She does not answer. The children come in—*JACK *with an armful of stockings,* MINNIE *with the basket of pegs.*

JACK: I believe it's freezing mother.

MINNIE: Mr Blackmore, could you shoot a rat an' hit it?

BLACKMORE (*laughing*): Shoot the lot of 'em, like a wink.

MRS HOLROYD: But you've had no tea. What an awful shame to keep you here!

BLACKMORE: Nay, I don't care. It never bothers me.

MRS HOLROYD: Then you're different from most men.

BLACKMORE: All men aren't alike, you know.

MRS HOLROYD: But do go and get some tea.

MINNIE (*plaintively*): Can't you stop, Mr Blackmore?

BLACKMORE: Why, Minnie?

MINNIE: So's we're not frightened. Yes, do. Will you?

BLACKMORE: Frightened of what?

MINNIE: 'Cause there's noises, an' rats—an' perhaps dad'll come home and shout.

BLACKMORE: But he'd shout more if I was here.

JACK: He doesn't when my uncle John's here. So you stop, an' perhaps he won't.

BLACKMORE: Don't you like him to shout when you're in bed?

They do not answer, but look seriously at him.

CURTAIN

SCENE TWO

The same scene, two hours later. The clothes are folded in little piles on the table and the sofa. MRS HOLROYD *is folding a thick flannel undervest or singlet which her husband wears in the pit and which has just dried on the fender.*

MRS HOLROYD (*to herself*): Now, thank goodness, they're all dried. It's only nine o'clock, so he won't be in for another two hours, the nuisance. (*She sits on the sofa, letting her arms hang down in dejection. After a minute or two she jumps up, to begin rudely dropping the piles of washed clothes in the basket.*) I don't care, I'm not going to let him have it all *his* way—no! (*She weeps a little, fiercely, drying her eyes on the edge of her white apron.*) Why should *I* put up with it all?—He can do what he likes. But I don't care, no, I don't——

She flings down the full clothes-basket, sits suddenly in the rocking-chair, and weeps. There is the sound of coarse, bursting laughter, in vain subdued, and a man's deep guffaws. Footsteps draw near. Suddenly the door opens, and a little, plump, pretty woman of thirty, in a close-fitting dress and a giddy, frilled bonnet of pink paper, stands perkily in the doorway. MRS HOLROYD *springs up; her small, sensitive nose is inflamed with weeping, her eyes are wet and flashing. She fronts the other woman.*

CLARA (*with a pert smile and a jerk of the head*): Good evenin'!

MRS HOLROYD: What do you want?

CLARA (*she has a Yorkshire accent*): Oh, we've not come beggin'—this is a visit.

She stuffs her handkerchief in front of her mouth in a little snorting burst of laughter. There is the sound of another woman behind going off into uncontrollable laughter, while a man guffaws.

MRS HOLROYD (*after a moment of impotence—tragically*): What——!

CLARA (*faltering slightly, affecting a polite tone*): We thought we'd just call——

She stuffs her handkerchief in front of her explosive laughter —the other woman shrieks again, beginning high, and running down the scale.

MRS HOLROYD: What do you mean?—What do you want here?

CLARA (*she bites her lip*): We don't want anything, thanks. We've just called. (*She begins to laugh again—so does the other.*) Well, I don't think much of the manners in this part of the country. (*She takes a few hesitating steps into the kitchen.*)

MRS HOLROYD (*trying to shut the door upon her*): No, you are not coming in.

CLARA (*preventing her closing the door*): Dear me, what a to-do! (*She struggles with the door. The other woman comes up to help; a man is seen in the background.*)

LAURA: My word, aren't we good enough to come in?

MRS HOLROYD, *finding herself confronted by what seems to her excitement a crowd, releases the door and draws back a little—almost in tears of anger.*

MRS HOLROYD: You have no business here. What do you want?

CLARA (*putting her bonnet straight and entering in brisk defiance*): I tell you we've only come to see you. (*She looks round the kitchen, then makes a gesture toward the arm-chair.*) Can I sit here? (*She plumps herself down.*) Rest for the weary.

A woman and a man have followed her into the room. LAURA *is highly coloured, stout, some forty years old, wears a blue paper bonnet, and looks like the landlady of a public-house. Both she and* CLARA *wear much jewellery.* LAURA *is well dressed in a blue cloth dress.* HOLROYD *is a big blond man. His cap is pushed back, and he looks rather tipsy and lawless. He has a heavy blond moustache. His jacket and trousers are black, his vest grey, and he wears a turn-down collar with dark bow.*

LAURA (*sitting down in a chair on right, her hand on her bosom, panting*): I've laughed till I feel fair bad.

CLARA: 'Aven't you got a drop of nothink to offer us, mester? Come, you are slow. I should 'ave thought a gentleman like you would have been out with the glasses afore we could have got breaths to ask you.

HOLROYD (*clumsily*): I dunna believe there's owt in th' 'ouse but a bottle of stout.

CLARA (*putting her hand on her stomach*): It feels as if th' kettle's going to boil over.

She stuffs her handkerchief in front of her mouth, throws back her head, and snorts with laughter, having now regained her confidence. LAURA *laughs in the last state of exhaustion, her hand on her breast.*

HOLROYD: Shall ta ha'e it then?

CLARA: What do you say, Laura—are you having a drop?

LAURA (*submissively, and naturally tongue-tied*): Well—I don't mind—I will if *you* do.

CLARA (*recklessly*): I think we'll 'ave a drop, Charlie, an' risk it. It'll 'appen hold the rest down.

There is a moment of silence, while HOLROYD *goes into the scullery.* CLARA *surveys the room and the dramatic pose of* MRS HOLROYD *curiously.*

HOLROYD (*suddenly*): Heh! What, come 'ere——!

There is a smash of pots, and a rat careers out of the scullery. LAURA, *the first to see it, utters a scream, but is fastened to her chair, unable to move.*

CLARA (*jumps up to the table, crying*): It's a rat—Oh, save us! (*She scrambles up, banging her head on the lamp, which swings violently.*)

MRS HOLROYD (*who, with a little shriek, jerks her legs up on to the sofa, where she was stiffly reclining, now cries in despairing falsetto, stretching forth her arms*): The lamp—mind, the lamp!

CLARA *steadies the lamp, and holds her hand to her head.*

HOLROYD (*coming from the scullery, a bottle of stout in his hand*): Where is he?

CLARA: I believe he's gone under the sofa. My, an' he's a thumper, if you like, as big as a rabbit.

    HOLROYD *advances cautiously toward the sofa.*

LAURA (*springing suddenly into life*): Hi, hi, let me go—let me go—Don't touch him—Where is he? (*She flees and scrambles on to* CLARA'S *arm-chair, catching hold of the latter's skirts.*)

CLARA: Hang off—do you want to have a body down—Mind, I tell you.

MRS HOLROYD (*bunched up on the sofa, with crossed hands holding her arms, fascinated, watches her husband as he approaches to stoop and attack the rat; she suddenly screams*): Don't, he'll fly at you.

HOLROYD: He'll not get a chance.

MRS HOLROYD: He will, he will—and they're poisonous! (*She ends on a very high note. Leaning forward on the sofa as far as she dares, she stretches out her arms to keep back her husband, who is about to kneel and search under the sofa for the rat.*)

HOLROYD: Come off, I canna see him.

MRS HOLROYD: I won't let you; he'll fly at you.

HOLROYD: I'll settle him——

MRS HOLROYD: Open the door and let him go.

HOLROYD: I shonna. I'll settle him. Shut thy claver. He'll non come anigh thee.

    He kneels down and begins to creep to the sofa. With a great bound, MRS HOLROYD *flies to the door and flings it open. Then she rushes back to the couch.*

CLARA: There he goes!

HOLROYD (*simultaneously*): Hi!—Ussza! (*He flings the bottle of stout out of the door.*)

LAURA (*piteously*): Shut the door, do.

    HOLROYD *rises, dusting his trousers knees, and closes the door.* LAURA *heavily descends and drops in the chair.*

CLARA: Here, come an' help us down, Charlie. Look at her; she's going off.

Though LAURA *is still purple-red, she sinks back in the chair.* HOLROYD *goes to the table.* CLARA *places her hands on his shoulders and jumps lightly down. Then she pushes* HOLROYD *with her elbow.*

Look sharp, get a glass of water.

She unfastens LAURA'S *collar and pulls off the paper bonnet.* MRS HOLROYD *sits up, straightens her clothing, and tries to look cold and contemptuous.* HOLROYD *brings a cup of water.* CLARA *sprinkles her friend's face.* LAURA *sighs and sighs again very deeply, then draws herself up painfully.*

CLARA *(tenderly)*: Do you feel any better—shall you have a drink of water?

LAURA mournfully shakes her head; CLARA *turns sharply to* HOLROYD.

She'll 'ave a drop o' something.

HOLROYD goes out. CLARA *meanwhile fans her friend with a handkerchief.* HOLROYD *brings stout. She pours out the stout, smells the glass, smells the bottle—then finally the cork.*

Eh, mester, it's all of a work—it's had a foisty cork.

At that instant the stairfoot door opens slowly, revealing the children—the girl peering over the boy's shoulder—both in white nightgowns. Everybody starts. LAURA *gives a little cry, presses her hand on her bosom, and sinks back, gasping.*

CLARA *(appealing and anxious, to* MRS HOLROYD*)*: You don't 'appen to 'ave a drop of brandy for her, do you, missis?

MRS HOLROYD rises coldly without replying, and goes to the stairfoot door where the children stand.

MRS HOLROYD *(sternly to the children)*: Go to bed!

JACK: What's a matter, mother?

MRS HOLROYD: Never you mind, go to bed!

CLARA *(appealingly)*: Be quick, missis.

MRS HOLROYD, glancing round, sees LAURA going purple, and runs past the children upstairs. The boy and girl sit on the

lowest stair. Their father goes out of the house, shamefaced.
MRS HOLROYD *runs downstairs with a little brandy in a large bottle.*

CLARA: Thanks, awfully. (*To* LAURA) Come on, try 'an drink a drop, there's a dear.

They administer brandy to LAURA. *The children sit watching, open-eyed. The girl stands up to look.*

MINNIE (*whispering*): I believe it's blue bonnet.

JACK (*whispering*): It isn't—she's in a fit.

MINNIE (*whispering*): Well, look under th' table—(JACK *peers under*)—there's 'er bonnet. (JACK *creeps forward.*) Come back, our Jack.

JACK (*returns with the bonnet*): It's all made of paper.

MINNIE: Let's have a look—it's stuck together, not sewed.

She tries it on. HOLROYD *enters—he looks at the child.*

MRS HOLROYD (*sharply, glancing round*): Take that off!

MINNIE *hurriedly takes the bonnet from her head. Her father snatches it from her and puts it on the fire.*

CLARA: There, you're coming round now, love.

MRS HOLROYD *turns away. She sees* HOLROYD'S *eyes on the brandy-bottle, and immediately removes it, corking it up*

MRS HOLROYD (*to* CLARA): You will not need this any more?

CLARA: No, thanks. I'm very much obliged.

MRS HOLROYD (*does not unbend, but speaks coldly to the children*): Come, this is no place for you—come back to bed.

MINNIE: No, mam, I don't want to.

MRS HOLROYD (*contralto*): Come along!

MINNIE: I'm frightened, mam.

MRS HOLROYD: Frightened, what of?

MINNIE: Oo, there *was* a row.

MRS HOLROYD (*taking* MINNIE *in her arms*): Did they frighten you, my pet? (*She kisses her.*)

JACK (*in a high whisper*): Mother, it's pink bonnet and blue bonnet, what was dancing.

MINNIE (*whimpering*): I don't want to go to bed, mam, I'm frightened.

CLARA (*who has pulled off her pink bonnet and revealed a jug-handle coiffure*): We're going now, duckie—you're not frightened of us, are you?

MRS HOLROYD *takes the girl away before she can answer.* JACK *lingers behind.*

HOLROYD: Now then, get off after your mother.

JACK (*taking no notice of his father*): I say, what's a dog's-nose?

CLARA *ups with her handkerchief and* LAURA *responds with a faint giggle.*

HOLROYD: Go thy ways upstairs.

CLARA: It's only a small whiskey with a spoonful of beer in it, my duck.

JACK: Oh!

CLARA: Come here, my duck, come on.

JACK *curious, advances.*

CLARA: You'll tell your mother we didn't mean no harm, won't you?

JACK (*touching her earrings*): What are they made of?

CLARA: They're only earrings. Don't you like them?

JACK: Um! (*He stands surveying her curiously. Then he touches a bracelet made of many little mosaic brooches.*) This is pretty, isn't it?

CLARA (*pleased*): Do you like it?

She takes it off. Suddenly MRS HOLROYD *is heard calling,* 'Jack, Jack!' CLARA *starts.*

HOLROYD: Now then, get off!

CLARA (*as* JACK *is reluctantly going*): Kiss me good night, duckie, an' give this to your sister, shall you?

She hands JACK *the mosaic bracelet. He takes it doubtfully. She kisses him.* HOLROYD *watches in silence.*

LAURA (*suddenly, pathetically*): Aren't you going to give me a kiss, an' all?

JACK *yields her his cheek, then goes.*

CLARA (*to* HOLROYD): Aren't they nice children?

HOLROYD: Ay.

CLARA (*briskly*): Oh, dear, you're very short, all of a sudden. Don't answer if it hurts you.

LAURA: My, isn't he different?

HOLROYD (*laughing forcedly*): I'm no different.

CLARA: Yes, you are. You shouldn't 'ave brought us if you was going to turn funny over it.

HOLROYD: I'm not funny.

CLARA: No, you're not. (*She begins to laugh.* LAURA *joins in in spite of herself.*) You're about as solemn as a roast potato. (*She flings up her hands, claps them down on her knees and sways up and down as she laughs,* LAURA *joining in, hand on breast.*) Are you ready to be mashed? (*She goes off again— then suddenly wipes the laughter off her mouth and is solemn.*) But look 'ere, this'll never do. Now I'm going to be quiet. (*She prims herself.*)

HOLROYD: Tha'd 'appen better.

CLARA: Oh, indeed! You think I've got to pull a mug to look decent? You'd have to pull a big un, at that rate.

She bubbles off, uncontrollably—shaking herself in exaspera- tion meanwhile. LAURA *joins in.* HOLROYD *leans over close to her*

HOLROYD: Tha's got plenty o' fizz in thee, seemly.

CLARA (*putting her hand on his face and pushing it aside, but leaving her hand over his cheek and mouth like a caress*): Don't, you've been drinking. (*She begins to laugh.*)

HOLROYD: Should we be goin' then?

CLARA: Where do you want to take us?

HOLROYD: Oh—you please yourself o' that! Come on wi' me.

CLARA (*sitting up prim*): Oh, indeed!

HOLROYD (*catching hold of her*): Come on, let's be movin'— (*he glances apprehensively at the stairs*).

CLARA: What's your hurry?

HOLROYD (*persuasively*): Yi, come on wi' thee.

CLARA: I don't think. (*She goes off, uncontrollably.*)

HOLROYD (*sitting on the table, just above her*): What's use o' sittin' 'ere?

CLARA: I'm very comfy: I thank thee.

HOLROYD: Tha'rt a baffling little 'ussy.

CLARA (*running her hand along his thigh*): Aren't you havin' nothing, my dear? (*Offers him her glass.*)

HOLROYD (*getting down from the table and putting his hand forcibly on her shoulder*): No. Come on, let's shift.

CLARA (*struggling*): Hands off!

    She fetches him a sharp slap across the face, MRS HOLROYD *is heard coming downstairs.* CLARA, *released, sits down, smoothing herself.* HOLROYD *looks evil. He goes out to the door.*

CLARA (*to* MRS HOLROYD, *penitently*): I don't know what you think of us, I'm sure.

MRS HOLROYD: I think nothing at all.

CLARA (*bubbling*): So you fix your thoughts elsewhere, do you? (*Suddenly changing to seriousness.*) No, but I *have* been awful to-night.

MRS HOLROYD (*contralto, emphatic*): I don't want to know anything about you. I shall be glad when you'll go.

CLARA: Turning-out time, Laura.

LAURA (*turtling*): I'm sorry, I'm sure.

CLARA: Never mind. But as true as I'm here, missis, I should never ha' come if I'd thought. But I had a drop—it all started with your husband sayin' he wasn't a married man.

LAURA (*laughing and wiping her eyes*): I've never knowed her to go off like it—it's after the time she's had.

CLARA: You know, my husband was a brute to me—an' I was in bed three month after he died. He was a brute, he was. This is the first time I've been out; it's a'most the first laugh I've had for a year.

LAURA: It's true, what she says. We thought she'd go out of 'er mind. She never spoke a word for a fortnight.

CLARA: Though he's only been dead for two months, he was a brute to me. I was as nice a young girl as you could wish when I married him and went to the Fleece Inn—I was.

LAURA: Killed hisself drinking. An' she's that excitable, she is. We s'll 'ave an awful time with 'er to-morrow, I know.

MRS HOLROYD (*coldly*): I don't know why I should hear all this.

CLARA: I know I must 'ave seemed awful. An' them children —aren't they nice little things, Laura?

LAURA: They are that.

HOLROYD (*entering from the door*): Hanna you about done theer?

CLARA: My word, if this is the way you treat a lady when she comes to see you. (*She rises.*)

HOLROYD: I'll see you down th' line.

CLARA: You're not coming a stride with us.

LAURA: We've got no hat, neither of us.

CLARA: We've got our own hair on our heads, at any rate. (*Drawing herself up suddenly in front of* MRS HOLROYD.) An' I've been educated at a boarding school as good as anybody. I can behave myself either in the drawing-room or in the kitchen as is fitting and proper. But if you'd buried a husband like mine, you wouldn't feel you'd much left to be proud of—an' you might go off occasionally.

MRS HOLROYD: I don't want to hear you.

CLARA (*bobbing a curtsy*): Sorry I spoke.

She goes out stiffly, followed by LAURA.

HOLROYD (*going forward*): You mun mind th' points down th' line.

CLARA'S VOICE: I thank thee, Charlie—mind thy own points.

He hesitates at the door—returns and sits down. There is silence in the room. HOLROYD *sits with his chin in his hand.* MRS HOLROYD *listens. The footsteps and voices of the two women die out. Then she closes the door.* HOLROYD *begins to unlace his boots.*

HOLROYD (*ashamed yet defiant, withal anxious to apologize*): Wheer's my slippers?

MRS HOLROYD *sits on the sofa with face averted and does not answer.*

HOLROYD: Dost hear? (*He pulls off his boots, noisily, and begins to hunt under the sofa.*) I canna find the things. (*No answer.*) Humph!—then I'll do be 'out 'em. (*He stumps about in his stockinged feet; going into the scullery, he brings out the loaf of bread; he returns into the scullery.*) Wheer's th' cheese? (*No answer—suddenly.*) God blast it! (*He hobbles into the kitchen.*) I've trod on that broken basin, an' cut my foot open. (MRS HOLROYD *refuses to take any notice. He sits down and looks at his sole—he pulls off his stocking and looks again.*) It's lamed me for life. (MRS HOLROYD *glances at the wound.*) Are 'na ter goin' ter get me öwt for it?

MRS HOLROYD: Psh!

HOLROYD: Oh, a' right then. (*He hops to the dresser, opens a drawer, and pulls out a white rag; he is about to tear it.*)

MRS HOLROYD (*snatching it from him*): Don't tear that!

HOLROYD (*shouting*): Then what the deuce am I to do? (MRS HOLROYD *sits stonily.*) Oh, a' right then! (*He hops back to his chair, sits down, and begins to pull on his stocking.*) A' right then—a' right then. (*In a fever of rage he begins pulling on his boots.*) I'll go where I *can* find a bit o' rag.

MRS HOLROYD: Yes, that's what you want! All you want is an excuse to be off again—'a bit of rag'!

HOLROYD (*shouting*): An' what man'd want to stop in wi' a woman sittin' as fow as a jackass, an' canna get a word from 'er edgeways.

MRS HOLROYD: Don't expect me to speak to you after to-night's show. How dare you bring them to my house, how dare you?

HOLROYD: They've non hurt your house, have they?

MRS HOLROYD: I wonder you dare to cross the doorstep.

HOLROYD: I s'll do what the deuce I like. They're as good as you are.

MRS HOLROYD (*stands speechless, staring at him; then low*): Don't you come near me again——

HOLROYD (*suddenly shouting, to get his courage up*): She's as good as you are, every bit of it.

MRS HOLROYD (*blazing*): Whatever I was and whatever I may be, don't you ever come near me again.

HOLROYD: What! I'll show thee. What's the hurt to you if a woman comes to the house? They're women as good as yourself, every whit of it.

MRS HOLROYD: Say no more. *Go* with them then, and don't come back.

HOLROYD: What! Yi, I will go, an' you s'll see. What! You think you're something, since your uncle left you that money, an' Blackymore puttin' you up to it. I can see your little game. I'm not as daft as you imagine. I'm no fool, I tell you.

MRS HOLROYD: No, you're not. You're a drunken beast, that's all you are.

HOLROYD: What, what—I'm what? I'll show you who's gaffer, though. (*He threatens her.*)

MRS HOLROYD (*between her teeth*): No, it's not going on. If *you* won't go, I will.

HOLROYD: Go then, for you've always been too big for your shoes, in my house——

MRS HOLROYD: Yes—I ought never to have looked at you. Only you showed a fair face then.

HOLROYD: What! What! We'll see who's master i' this house. I tell you, I'm goin' to put a stop to it. (*He brings his fist down on the table with a bang.*) It's going to stop. (*He bangs the table again.*) I've put up with it long enough. Do you think I'm a dog in the house, an' not a man, do you——

MRS HOLROYD: A dog would be better.

HOLROYD: Oh! Oh! Then we'll see. We'll see who's the dog and who isna. We're goin' to see. (*He bangs the table.*)

MRS HOLROYD: Stop thumping that table! You've wakened those children once, you and your trollops.

HOLROYD: I shall do what the deuce I like!

MRS HOLROYD: No more, you won't, no more. I've stood this long enough. Now I'm going. As for you—you've got a red face where she slapped you. Now go to her.

HOLROYD: What? What?

MRS HOLROYD: For I'm sick of the sights and sounds of you.

HOLROYD (*bitterly*): By God, an' I've known it a long time.

MRS HOLROYD: You have, and it's true.

HOLROYD: An' I know who it is th'rt hankerin' after.

MRS HOLROYD: I only want to be rid of you.

HOLROYD: I know it mighty well. But *I* know him!

    MRS HOLROYD *sinking down on the sofa, suddenly begins to sob half-hysterically.* HOLROYD *watches her. As suddenly, she dries her eyes.*

MRS HOLROYD: Do you think I care about what you say? (*Suddenly.*) Oh, I've had enough. I've tried, I've tried for years, for the children's sakes. Now I've had enough of your shame and disgrace.

HOLROYD: Oh, indeed!

MRS HOLROYD (*her voice is dull and inflexible*): I've had enough. Go out again after those trollops—leave me alone. I've had enough. (HOLROYD *stands looking at her.*) Go, I mean it, go out again. And if you never come back again, I'm glad. I've had enough. (*She keeps her face averted, will not look at him, her attitude expressing thorough weariness.*)

HOLROYD: All right then!

    He hobbles, in unlaced boots, to the door. Then he turns to look at her. She turns herself still farther away, so that her back is towards him. He goes.

CURTAIN

ACT TWO

The scene is the same, two hours later. The cottage is in darkness, save for the firelight. On the table is spread a newspaper. A cup and saucer, a plate, a piece of bacon in the frying tin are on the newspaper ready for the miner's breakfast. MRS HOLROYD *has gone to bed. There is a noise of heavy stumbling down the three steps outside.*

BLACKMORE'S VOICE: Steady now, steady. It's all in darkness. Missis!—Has she gone to bed?
   He tries the latch—shakes the door.

HOLROYD'S VOICE (*He is drunk*): Her's locked me out. Let me smash that bloody door in. Come out—come out—ussza! (*He strikes a heavy blow on the door. There is a scuffle.*)

BLACKMORE'S VOICE: Hold on a bit—what're you doing?

HOLROYD'S VOICE: I'm smashing that blasted door in.

MRS HOLROYD (*appearing and suddenly drawing the bolts, flinging the door open*): What do you think you're doing?

HOLROYD (*lurching into the room, snarling*): What? What? Tha thought tha'd play thy monkey tricks on me, did ter? (*Shouting.*) But I'm going to show thee. (*He lurches at her threateningly; she recoils.*)

BLACKMORE (*seizing him by the arm*): Here, here—! Come and sit down and be quiet.

HOLROYD (*snarling at him*): What?—What? An' what's thäigh got ter do wi' it. (*Shouting.*) What's thäigh got ter do wi' it?

BLACKMORE: Nothing—nothing; but it's getting late, and you want your supper.

HOLROYD (*shouting*): I want nöwt. I'm allowed nöwt in this

'ouse. (*Shouting louder.*) 'Er begrudges me ivry morsel I ha'e.

MRS HOLROYD: Oh, what a story!

HOLROYD (*shouting*): It's the truth, an' you know it.

BLACKMORE (*conciliatory*): You'll rouse the children. You'll rouse the children, at this hour.

HOLROYD (*suddenly quiet*): Not me—not if I know it. *I* shan't disturb 'em—bless 'em.

He staggers to his arm-chair and sits heavily.

BLACKMORE: Shall I light the lamp?

MRS HOLROYD: No, don't trouble. Don't stay any longer, there's no need.

BLACKMORE (*quietly*): I'll just see it's all right.

He proceeds in silence to light the lamp, HOLROYD *is seen dropping forward in his chair. He has a cut on his cheek.* MRS HOLROYD *is in an old-fashioned dressing-gown.* BLACKMORE *has an overcoat buttoned up to his chin. There is a very large lump of coal on the red fire.*

MRS HOLROYD: Don't stay any longer.

BLACKMORE: I'll see it's all right.

MRS HOLROYD: I shall be all right. He'll go to sleep now.

BLACKMORE: But he can't go like that.

MRS HOLROYD: What has he done to his face?

BLACKMORE: He had a row with Jim Goodwin.

MRS HOLROYD: What about?

BLACKMORE: I don't know.

MRS HOLROYD: The beast!

BLACKMORE: By Jove, and isn't he a weight! He's getting fat, must be——

MRS HOLROYD: He's big made—he has a big frame.

BLACKMORE: Whatever he is, it took me all my time to get him home. I thought I'd better keep an eye on him. I knew you'd be worrying. So I sat in the smoke-room and waited for him. Though it's a dirty hole—and dull as hell.

MRS HOLROYD: Why did you bother?

BLACKMORE: Well, I thought you'd be upset about him. I

had to drink three whiskies—had to, in all conscience— (*smiling*).

MRS HOLROYD: I don't want to be the ruin of you.

BLACKMORE (*smiling*): Don't you? I thought he'd pitch forward on to the lines and crack his skull.

HOLROYD *has been sinking farther and farther forward in drunken sleep. He suddenly jerks too far and is awakened. He sits upright, glaring fiercely and dazedly at the two, who instantly cease talking.*

HOLROYD (*to* BLACKMORE): What are thäigh doin' 'ere?

BLACKMORE: Why, I came along with you.

HOLROYD: Thou'rt a liar, I'm only just come in.

MRS HOLROYD (*coldly*): He is no liar at all. He brought you home because you were too drunk to come yourself.

HOLROYD (*starting up*): Thou'rt a liar! I niver set eyes on him this night, afore now.

MRS HOLROYD (*with a 'Pf' of contempt*): You don't know what you *have* done to-night.

HOLROYD (*shouting*): I s'll not ha'e it, I tell thee.

MRS HOLROYD: Psh!

HOLROYD: I s'll not ha'e it. I s'll ha'e no carryin's on i' my 'ouse——

MRS HOLROYD (*shrugging her shoulders*): Talk when you've got some sense.

HOLROYD (*fiercely*): I've as much sense as thäigh. Am I a fool? Canna I see? What's *he* doin' here then, answer me that. What——?

MRS HOLROYD: Mr Blackmore came to bring *you* home because you were *too* drunk to find your own way. And this is the thanks he gets.

HOLROYD (*contemptuously*): Blackymore, Blackymore It's him tha cuts thy cloth by, is it?

MRS HOLROYD (*hotly*): You don't know what you're talking about, so keep your tongue still.

HOLROYD (*bitingly*): I don't know what I'm talking about—

I don't know what I'm talking about—don't I? An' what about him standing there then, if I don't know what I'm talking about?—What?

BLACKMORE: You've been to sleep, Charlie, an' forgotten I came in with you, not long since.

HOLROYD: I'm not daft, I'm not a fool. I've got eyes in my head and sense. You needn't try to get over me. I know what you're up to.

BLACKMORE (*flushing*): It's a bit off to talk to me like that, Charlie, I must say.

HOLROYD: I'm not good enough for 'er. She wants Mr Blackymore. He's a gentleman, he is. Now we have it all; now we understand.

MRS HOLROYD: I wish you understood enough to keep your tongue still.

HOLROYD: What? What? I'm to keep my tongue still, am I? An' what about *Mr Blackymore*?

MRS HOLROYD (*fiercely*): Stop your mouth, you—you vulgar, low-minded brute.

HOLROYD: Am I? Am I? An' what are you? What tricks are you up to, an' all? But that's all right—that's all right. (*Shouting.*) That's all right, if it's *you*.

BLACKMORE: I think I'd better go. You seem to enjoy—er—er—calumniating your wife.

HOLROYD (*mockingly*): Calamniating—calamniating—I'll give you calamniating, you mealy-mouthed jockey: I'll give you calamniating.

BLACKMORE: I think you've said about enough.

HOLROYD: 'Ave I, 'ave I? Yer flimsy jack—'ave I? (*In a sudden burst.*) But I've not done wi' thee yet?

BLACKMORE (*ironically*): No, and you haven't.

HOLROYD (*shouting—pulling himself up from the arm-chair*): I'll show thee—I'll show thee.

BLACKMORE *laughs.*

HOLROYD: Yes!—yes, my young monkey. It's thäigh, is it?

BLACKMORE: Yes, it's *me*.

HOLROYD (*shouting*): An' I'll ma'e thee wish it worn't, I will. What—? What? Tha'd come slivin' round here, would ta? (*He lurches forward at* BLACKMORE *with clenched fist.*)

MRS HOLROYD: Drunken, drunken fool—oh, don't.

HOLROYD (*turning to her*): What?

She puts up her hands before her face. BLACKMORE *seizes the upraised arm and swings* HOLROYD *round.*

BLACKMORE (*in a towering passion*): Mind what tha'rt doing!

HOLROYD (*turning fiercely on him—incoherent*): Wha'— wha'——!

He aims a heavy blow. BLACKMORE *evades it, so that he is struck on the side of the chest. Suddenly he shows his teeth. He raises his fists ready to strike* HOLROYD *when the latter stands to advantage.*

MRS HOLROYD (*rushing upon* BLACKMORE): No, no! Oh, no!

She flies and opens the door, and goes out. BLACKMORE *glances after her, then at* HOLROYD, *who is preparing, like a bull, for another charge. The young man's face lights up.*

HOLROYD: Wha'—wha'——!

As he advances, BLACKMORE *quickly retreats out-of-doors.* HOLROYD *plunges upon him,* BLACKMORE *slips behind the door-jamb, puts out his foot, and trips* HOLROYD *with a crash upon the brick yard.*

MRS HOLROYD: Oh, what has he done to himself?

BLACKMORE (*thickly*): Tumbled over himself.

HOLROYD is seen struggling to rise, and is heard incoherently cursing.

MRS HOLROYD: Aren't you going to get him up?

BLACKMORE: What for?

MRS HOLROYD: But what shall we do?

BLACKMORE: Let him go to hell.

HOLROYD, who has subsided, begins to snarl and struggle again.

MRS HOLROYD (*in terror*): He's getting up.

BLACKMORE: All right, let him.

MRS HOLROYD *looks at* BLACKMORE, *suddenly afraid of him also.*

HOLROYD (*in a last frenzy*): I'll show thee—I'll——

He raises himself up, and is just picking his balance when BLACKMORE, *with a sudden light kick, sends him sprawling again. He is seen on the edge of the light to collapse into stupor.*

MRS HOLROYD: He'll kill you, he'll kill you!

BLACKMORE *laughs short.*

MRS HOLROYD: Would you believe it! Oh, isn't it awful! (*She begins to weep in a little hysteria;* BLACKMORE *stands with his back leaning on the doorway, grinning in a strained fashion.*) Is he hurt, do you think?

BLACKMORE: I don't know—I should think not.

MRS HOLROYD: I wish he was dead; I do, with all my heart.

BLACKMORE: Do you? (*He looks at her quickly; she wavers and shrinks; he begins to smile strainedly as before.*) You don't know *what* you wish, or what you want.

MRS HOLROYD (*troubled*): Do you think I could get past him to come inside?

BLACKMORE: I should think so.

MRS HOLROYD, *silent and troubled, manoeuvres in the doorway, stepping over her husband's feet, which lie on the threshold.*

BLACKMORE: Why, you've got no shoes and stockings on!

MRS HOLROYD: No. (*She enters the house and stands trembling before the fire.*)

BLACKMORE (*following her*): Are you cold?

MRS HOLROYD: A little—with standing on the yard.

BLACKMORE: What a shame!

She, uncertain of herself, sits down. He drops on one knee, awkwardly, and takes her feet in his hands.

MRS HOLROYD: Don't—no, don't!

BLACKMORE: They are frightfully cold. (*He remains, with head sunk, for some moments, then slowly rises.*) Damn him!

They look at each other; then, at the same time, turn away.

MRS HOLROYD: We can't leave him lying there.

BLACKMORE: No—no! I'll bring him in.

MRS HOLROYD: But——!

BLACKMORE: He won't wake again. The drink will have got hold of him by now. (*He hesitates.*) Could you take hold of his feet—he's so heavy.

MRS HOLROYD: Yes.

They go out and are seen stooping over HOLROYD.

BLACKMORE: Wait, wait, till I've got him—half a minute.

MRS HOLROYD *backs in first. They carry* HOLROYD *in and lay him on the sofa.*

MRS HOLROYD: Doesn't he look awful?

BLACKMORE: It's more mark than mar. It isn't much, really.

He is busy taking off HOLROYD'S *collar and tie, unfastening the waistcoat, the braces and the waist buttons of the trousers; he then proceeds to unlace the drunken man's boots.*

MRS HOLROYD (*who has been watching closely*): I shall never get him upstairs.

BLACKMORE: He can sleep here, with a rug or something to cover him. *You* don't want him—upstairs?

MRS HOLROYD: Never again.

BLACKMORE (*after a moment or two of silence*): He'll be all right down here. Have you got a rug?

MRS HOLROYD: Yes.

She goes upstairs. BLACKMORE *goes into the scullery, returning with a ladling can and towel. He gets hot water from the boiler. Then, kneeling down, he begins to wipe the drunken man's face lightly with the flannel, to remove the blood and dirt.*

MRS HOLROYD (*returning*): What are you doing?

BLACKMORE: Only wiping his face to get the dirt out.

MRS HOLROYD: I wonder if he'd do as much for you.

BLACKMORE: I hope not.

MRS HOLROYD: Isn't he horrible, horrible——

BLACKMORE (*looks up at her*): Don't look at him then.

MRS HOLROYD: I can't take it in, it's too much.

BLACKMORE: He won't wake. I will stay with you.

MRS HOLROYD (*earnestly*): No—oh, no.

BLACKMORE: There will be the drawn sword between us. (*He indicates the figure of* HOLROYD, *which lies, in effect, as a barrier between them.*)

MRS HOLROYD (*blushing*): Don't!

BLACKMORE: I'm sorry.

MRS HOLROYD (*after watching him for a few moments lightly wiping the sleeping man's face with a towel*): I wonder you can be so careful over him.

BLACKMORE (*quietly*): It's only because he's helpless.

MRS HOLROYD: But why should you love him ever so little?

BLACKMORE: I don't—only he's helpless. Five minutes since I could have killed him.

MRS HOLROYD: Well, I don't understand you men.

BLACKMORE: Why?

MRS HOLROYD: I don't know.

BLACKMORE: I thought as I stood in that doorway, and he was trying to get up—I wished as hard as I've ever wished anything in my life——

MRS HOLROYD: What?

BLACKMORE: That I'd killed him. I've never wished anything so much in my life—if wishes were anything.

MRS HOLROYD: Don't, it *does* sound awful.

BLACKMORE: I *could* have done it, too. He ought to be dead.

MRS HOLROYD (*pleading*): No, don't! You know you don't mean it, and you make me feel so awful.

BLACKMORE: I do mean it. It is simply true, what I say.

MRS HOLROYD: But don't say it.

BLACKMORE: No?

MRS HOLROYD: No, we've had enough.

BLACKMORE: Give me the rug.

She hands him it, and he tucks HOLROYD *up.*

MRS HOLROYD: You only do it to play on my feelings.

BLACKMORE (*laughing shortly*): And now give me a pillow—thanks.

There is a pause—both look at the sleeping man.

BLACKMORE: I suppose you're fond of him, really.

MRS HOLROYD: No more.

BLACKMORE: You *were* fond of him?

MRS HOLROYD: I was—yes.

BLACKMORE: What did you like in him?

MRS HOLROYD (*uneasily*): I don't know.

BLACKMORE: I suppose you really care about him, even now?

MRS HOLROYD: Why are you so sure of it?

BLACKMORE: Because I think it is so.

MRS HOLROYD: I did care for him—now he has destroyed it——

BLACKMORE: I don't believe he can destroy it.

MRS HOLROYD (*with a short laugh*): Don't you? When you are married you try. You'll find it isn't so hard.

BLACKMORE: But what did you like in him—because he was good-looking, and strong, and that?

MRS HOLROYD: I liked that as well. But if a man makes a nuisance of himself, his good looks are ugly to you, and his strength loathsome. Do you think I *care* about a man because he's got big fists, when he is a coward in his real self?

BLACKMORE: Is he a coward?

MRS HOLROYD: He *is*—a pettifogging, paltry one.

BLACKMORE: And so you've really done with him?

MRS HOLROYD: I have.

BLACKMORE: And what are you going to do?

MRS HOLROYD: I don't know.

BLACKMORE: I suppose nothing. You'll just go on—even if you've done with him—you'll go on with him.

There is a long pause

BLACKMORE: But was there nothing else in him but his muscles and his good looks to attract you to him?

MRS HOLROYD: Why? What does it matter?

BLACKMORE: What did you *think* he was?

MRS HOLROYD: Why must we talk about him?

BLACKMORE: Because I can never quite believe you.

MRS HOLROYD: I can't help whether you believe it or not.

BLACKMORE: Are you just in a rage with him, because of to-night?

MRS HOLROYD: I know, to-night finished it. But it was never right between us.

BLACKMORE: Never?

MRS HOLROYD: Not once. And then to-night—no, it's too much; I can't stand any more of it.

BLACKMORE: I suppose he got tipsy. Then he said he wasn't a married man—vowed he wasn't, to those paper bonnets. They found out he was, and said he was frightened of his wife getting to know. Then he said they should all go to supper at his house—I suppose they came out of mischief.

MRS HOLROYD: He did it to insult me.

BLACKMORE: Oh, he was a bit tight—you can't say it was deliberate.

MRS HOLROYD: No, but it shows how he feels towards me. The feeling comes out in drink.

BLACKMORE: How does he feel toward you?

MRS HOLROYD: He wants to insult me, and humiliate me, in every moment of his life. Now I simply despise him.

BLACKMORE: You really don't care any more about him?

MRS HOLROYD: No.

BLACKMORE (*hesitates*): And you would leave him?

MRS HOLROYD: I would leave him, and not care *that* about him any more. (*She snaps her fingers.*)

BLACKMORE: Will you come with me?

MRS HOLROYD (*after a reluctant pause*): Where?

BLACKMORE: To Spain: I can any time have a job there, in a decent part. You could take the children.

The figure of the sleeper stirs uneasily—they watch him.

BLACKMORE: Will you?

MRS HOLROYD: When would you go?

BLACKMORE: To-morrow, if you like.

MRS HOLROYD: But why do you want to saddle yourself with me and the children?

BLACKMORE: Because I want to.

MRS HOLROYD: But you don't love me?

BLACKMORE: Why don't I?

MRS HOLROYD: You don't.

BLACKMORE: I don't know about that. I don't know anything about love. Only I've gone on for a year, now, and it's got stronger and stronger——

MRS HOLROYD: What has?

BLACKMORE: This—this wanting you, to live with me. I took no notice of it for a long time. Now I can't get away from it, at no hour and nohow. (*He still avoids direct contact with her.*)

MRS HOLROYD: But you'd *like* to get away from it.

BLACKMORE: I hate a mess of any sort. But if you'll come away with me—you and the children——

MRS HOLROYD: But I couldn't—you don't love me——

BLACKMORE: I don't know what you mean by I don't love you.

MRS HOLROYD: I can feel it.

BLACKMORE: And do you love *me*? (*A pause.*)

MRS HOLROYD: I don't know. Everything is so—so——
    There is a long pause.

BLACKMORE: How old are you?

MRS HOLROYD: Thirty-two.

BLACKMORE: I'm twenty-seven.

MRS HOLROYD: And have you never been in love?

BLACKMORE: I don't think so. I don't know.

MRS HOLROYD: But you must know. I must go and shut that door that keeps clicking.
    She rises to go upstairs, making a clatter at the stairfoot door.

The noise rouses her husband. As she goes upstairs, he moves, makes coughing sounds, turns over, and then suddenly sits upright, gazing at BLACKMORE. *The latter sits perfectly still on the sofa, his head dropped, hiding his face. His hands are clasped. They remain thus for a minute.*

HOLROYD: Hello! (*He stares fixedly.*) Hello! (*His tone is undecided, as if he mistrusts himself.*) What are—who are ter? (BLACKMORE *does not move;* HOLROYD *stares blankly; he then turns and looks at the room.*) Well, I dunna know.

He staggers to his feet, clinging to the table, and goes groping to the stairs. They creak loudly under his weight. A door-latch is heard to click. In a moment MRS HOLROYD *comes quickly downstairs.*

BLACKMORE: Has he gone to bed?

MRS HOLROYD (*nodding*): Lying on the bed.

BLACKMORE: Will he settle now?

MRS HOLROYD: I don't know. He is like that sometimes. He will have delirium tremens if he goes on.

BLACKMORE (*softly*): You can't stay with him, you know.

MRS HOLROYD: And the children?

BLACKMORE: We'll take them.

MRS HOLROYD: Oh!

Her face puckers to cry. Suddenly he starts up and puts his arms round her, holding her protectively and gently, very caressingly. She clings to him. They are silent for some moments.

BLACKMORE (*struggling, in an altered voice*): Look at me and kiss me.

Her sobs are heard distinctly, BLACKMORE *lays his hand on her cheek, caressing her always with his hand.*

BLACKMORE: My God, but I hate him! I wish either he was dead or me. (MRS HOLROYD *hides against him; her sobs cease; after a while he continues in the same murmuring fashion.*) It can't go on like it any more. I feel as if I should come in two. I can't keep away from you. I simply can't. Come with me. Come with me and leave him. If you knew what a hell it is for me to have you here—and to see him. I can't go without you, I can't. It's been hell every moment for six months now. You say I don't love you. Perhaps I don't, for all I know about it. But oh, my God, don't keep me like it any longer. Why should *he* have you—and I've never had anything.

MRS HOLROYD: Have you never loved anybody?

BLACKMORE: No—I've tried. Kiss me of your own wish—will you?

MRS HOLROYD: I don't know.

BLACKMORE (*after a pause*): Let's break clear. Let's go right away. Do you care for me?

MRS HOLROYD: I don't know. (*She loosens herself, rises dumbly.*)

BLACKMORE: When do you think you *will* know?

  She sits down helplessly.

MRS HOLROYD: I don't know.

BLACKMORE: Yes, you do know, really. If he was dead, should you marry me?

MRS HOLROYD: Don't say it——

BLACKMORE: Why not? If wishing of mine would kill him, he'd soon be out of the way.

MRS HOLROYD: But the children!

BLACKMORE: I'm fond of them. I shall have good money.

MRS HOLROYD: But he's their father.

BLACKMORE: What does that mean——?

MRS HOLROYD: Yes, I know—(*a pause*) but——

BLACKMORE: Is it *him* that keeps you?

MRS HOLROYD: No.

BLACKMORE: Then come with me. Will you? (*He stands waiting for her; then he turns and takes his overcoat; pulls it on, leaving the collar turned up, ceasing to twist his cap.*) Well—will you tell me to-morrow?

  She goes forward and flings her arms round his neck. He suddenly kisses her passionately.

MRS HOLROYD: But I ought not. (*She draws away a little; he will not let her go.*)

BLACKMORE: Yes, it's all right. (*He holds her close.*)

MRS HOLROYD: Is it?

BLACKMORE: Yes, it is. It's all right.

He kisses her again. She releases herself but holds his hand. They keep listening.

MRS HOLROYD: Do you love me?

BLACKMORE: What do you ask for?

MRS HOLROYD: Have I hurt you these months?

BLACKMORE: *You* haven't. And I don't care what it's been if you'll come with me. (*There is a noise upstairs and they wait.*) You *will* soon, won't you?

She kisses him.

MRS HOLROYD: He's not safe. (*She disengages herself and sits on the sofa.*)

BLACKMORE (*takes a place beside her, holding her hand in both his*): You should have waited for me.

MRS HOLROYD: How wait?

BLACKMORE: And not have married him.

MRS HOLROYD: I might never have known you—I married him to get out of my place.

BLACKMORE: Why?

MRS HOLROYD: I was left an orphan when I was six. My Uncle John brought me up, in the Coach and Horses at Rainsworth. He'd got no children. He was good to me, but he drank. I went to Mansfield Grammar School. Then he fell out with me because I wouldn't wait in the bar, and I went as nursery governess to Berryman's. And I felt I'd nowhere to go. I belonged to nowhere, and nobody cared about me, and men came after me, and I hated it. So to get out of it, I married the first man that turned up.

BLACKMORE: And you never cared about him?

MRS HOLROYD: Yes, I did. I did care about him. I wanted to be a wife to him. But there's nothing at the bottom of him, if you know what I mean. You can't *get* anywhere with him. There's just his body and nothing else. Nothing that keeps him, no anchor, no roots, nothing satisfying. It's a horrible feeling there is about him, that nothing is safe or permanent—nothing is anything——

BLACKMORE: And do you think you can trust *me*?

MRS HOLROYD: I think you're different from him.

BLACKMORE: Perhaps I'm not.

MRS HOLROYD (*warmly*): You are.

BLACKMORE: At any rate, we'll see. You'll come on Saturday to London?

MRS HOLROYD: Well, you see, there's my money. I haven't got it yet. My uncle has left me about a hundred and twenty pounds.

BLACKMORE: Well, see the lawyer about it as soon as you can. I can let you have have some money if you want any. But don't let us wait after Saturday.

MRS HOLROYD: But isn't it wrong?

BLACKMORE: Why, if you don't care for him, and the children are miserable between the two of you—which they are——

MRS HOLROYD: Yes.

BLACKMORE: Well, then I see no wrong. As for him—he would go one way, and only one way, whatever you do. Damn him, he doesn't matter.

MRS HOLROYD: No.

BLACKMORE: Well, then—have done with it. Can't you cut clean of him? Can't you now?

MRS HOLROYD: And then—the children——

BLACKMORE: They'll be all right with me and you—won't they?

MRS HOLROYD: Yes——

BLACKMORE: Well, then. Now, come and have done with it. We can't keep on being ripped in two like this. We need never hear of him any more.

MRS HOLROYD: Yes—I love you. I do love you——

BLACKMORE: Oh, my God! (*He speaks with difficulty—embracing her.*)

MRS HOLROYD: When I look at him, and then at you—ha—(*She gives a short laugh*).

BLACKMORE: He's had all the chance—it's only fair—Lizzie——

MRS HOLROYD: My love.

There is silence. He keeps his arm round her. After hesitating, he picks up his cap.

BLACKMORE: I'll go then—at any rate. Shall you come with me?

She follows him to the door.

MRS HOLROYD: I'll come on Saturday.

BLACKMORE: Not now?

CURTAIN

ACT THREE

*Scene, the same. Time, the following evening, about seven o'clock.
The table is half-laid, with a large cup and saucer, plate, etc.,
ready for HOLROYD'S dinner, which, like all miners, he has
when he comes home between four and five o'clock. On the other
half of the table MRS HOLROYD is ironing. On the hearth
stand newly baked loaves of bread. The irons hang at the fire.
JACK, with a bowler hat hanging at the back of his head,
parades up to the sofa, on which stands MINNIE engaged in
dusting a picture. She has a soiled white apron tied behind her,
to make a long skirt.*

JACK: Good mornin', missis. Any scissors or knives to grind?

MINNIE (*peering down from the sofa*): Oh, I can't be bothered
to come downstairs. Call another day.

JACK: I shan't.

MINNIE (*keeping up her part*): Well, I can't come down now.
(JACK *stands irresolute.*) Go on, you have to go and steal
the baby.

JACK: I'm not.

MINNIE: Well, you can steal the eggs out of the fowl-house.

JACK: I'm not.

MINNIE: Then I shan't play with you.

    JACK *takes off his bowler hat and flings it on the sofa; tears
come in* MINNIE'S *eyes.*

    Now I'm *not* friends. (*She surveys him ruefully; after a few
moments of silence she clambers down and goes to her mother.*)
Mam, he won't play with me.

MRS HOLROYD (*crossly*): Why don't you play with her? If
you begin bothering, you must go to bed.

JACK: Well, I don't want to play.

MRS HOLROYD: Then you must go to bed.

JACK: I don't want to.

MRS HOLROYD: Then what do you want, I should like to know?

MINNIE: I wish my father'd come.

JACK: I do.

MRS HOLROYD: I suppose he thinks he's paying me out. This is the third time this week he's slunk past the door and gone down to Old Brinsley instead of coming in to his dinner. He'll be as drunk as a lord when he does come. *The children look at her plaintively.*

MINNIE: Isn't he a nuisance?

JACK: I hate him. I wish he'd drop down th' pit-shaft.

MRS HOLROYD: Jack!—I never heard such a thing in my life! You mustn't say such things—it's wicked.

JACK: Well, I do.

MRS HOLROYD (*loudly*): I won't have it. He's your father, remember.

JACK (*in a high voice*): Well, he's always comin' home an' shoutin' an' bangin' on the table. (*He is getting tearful and defiant.*)

MRS HOLROYD: Well, you mustn't take any notice of him.

MINNIE (*wistfully*): 'Appen if you said something nice to him, mother, he'd happen go to bed, and not shout.

JACK: I'd hit him in the mouth.

MRS HOLROYD: Perhaps we'll go to another country, away from him—should we?

JACK: In a ship, mother?

MINNIE: In a ship, mam?

MRS HOLROYD: Yes, in a big ship, where it's blue sky, and water and palm-trees, and——

MINNIE: An' dates——?

JACK: When should we go?

MRS HOLROYD: Some day.

MINNIE: But who'd work for us? Who should we have for father?

JACK: You don't want a father. I can go to work for us.

MRS HOLROYD: I've got a lot of money now, that your uncle left me.

MINNIE (*after a general thoughtful silence*): An' would my father stop here?

MRS HOLROYD: Oh, he'd be all right.

MINNIE: But who would he live with?

MRS HOLROYD: I don't know—one of his paper bonnets, if he likes.

MINNIE: Then she could have her old bracelet back, couldn't she?

MRS HOLROYD: Yes—there it is on the candlestick, waiting for her.

> *There is a sound of footsteps—then a knock at the door. The children start.*

MINNIE (*in relief*): Here he is.

> MRS HOLROYD *goes to the door.* BLACKMORE *enters.*

BLACKMORE: It is foggy to-night—Hello, aren't you youngsters gone to bed?

MINNIE: No, my father's not come home yet.

BLACKMORE (*turning to* MRS HOLROYD): Did he go to work then, after last night?

MRS HOLROYD: I suppose so. His pit things were gone when I got up. I never thought he'd go.

BLACKMORE: And he took his snap as usual?

MRS HOLROYD: Yes, just as usual. I suppose he's gone to the New Inn. He'd say to himself he'd pay me out. That's what he always does say, 'I'll pay thee out for that bit—I'll ma'e thee regret it.'

JACK: We're going to leave him.

BLACKMORE: So you think he's at the New Inn?

MRS HOLROYD: I'm sure he is—and he'll come when he's full. He'll have a bout now, you'll see.

MINNIE: Go and fetch him, Mr Blackmore.

JACK: My mother says we shall go in a ship and leave him.

BLACKMORE (*after looking keenly at* JACK: *to* MRS HOLROYD):
Shall I go and see if he's at the New Inn?

MRS HOLROYD: No—perhaps you'd better not——

BLACKMORE: Oh, he shan't see me. I can easily manage
that.

JACK: Fetch him, Mr Blackmore.

BLACKMORE: All right, Jack. (*To* MRS HOLROYD.) Shall I?
        BLACKMORE *goes out.*

MRS HOLROYD: We're always pulling on you—— But yes,
do!

JACK: I wonder how long he'll be.

MRS HOLROYD: You come and go to bed now: you'd better
be out of the way when he comes in.

MINNIE: And you won't say anything to him, mother, will
you?

MRS HOLROYD: What do you mean?

MINNIE: You won't begin of him—row him.

MRS HOLROYD: Is he to have all his own way? What *would*
he be like, if I didn't row him?

JACK: But it doesn't matter, mother, if we're going to leave
him——

MINNIE: But Mr Blackmore'll come back, won't he, mam,
and dad won't shout before him?

MRS HOLROYD (*beginning to undress the children*): Yes, he'll
come back.

MINNIE: Mam—could I have that bracelet to go to bed with?

MRS HOLROYD: Come and say your prayers.
    They kneel, muttering in their mother's apron.

MINNIE (*suddenly lifting her head*): Can I, mam?

MRS HOLROYD (*trying to be stern*): Have you finished your
prayers?

MINNIE: Yes.

MRS HOLROYD: If you want it—beastly thing! (*She reaches
the bracelet down from the mantelpiece.*) Your father must
have put it up there—I don't know where I left it. I sup-

pose he'd think I was proud of it and wanted it for an ornament.

MINNIE *gloats over it.* MRS HOLROYD *lights a candle and they go upstairs. After a few moments the outer door opens, and there enters an old woman. She is of middling stature and wears a large grey shawl over her head. After glancing sharply round the room, she advances to the fire, warms herself, then, taking off her shawl, sits in the rocking-chair. As she hears* MRS HOLROYD'S *footsteps, she folds her hands and puts on a lachrymose expression, turning down the corners of her mouth and arching her eyebrows.*

MRS HOLROYD: Hello, mother, is it you?

GRANDMOTHER: Yes, it's me. Haven't you finished ironing?

MRS HOLROYD: Not yet.

GRANDMOTHER: You'll have your irons red-hot.

MRS HOLROYD: Yes, I s'll have to stand them to cool. (*She does so, and moves about at her ironing.*)

GRANDMOTHER: And you don't know what's become of Charles?

MRS HOLROYD: Well, he's not come home from work yet. I supposed he was at the New Inn—Why?

GRANDMOTHER: That young electrician come knocking asking if I knew where he was. 'Eh,' I said, 'I've not set eyes on him for over a week—nor his wife neither, though they pass th' garden gate every time they go out. I know nowt on 'im.' I axed him what was the matter, so he said Mrs Holroyd was anxious because he'd not come home, so I thought I'd better come and see. Is there anything up?

MRS HOLROYD: No more than I've told you.

GRANDMOTHER: It's a rum 'un, if he's neither in the New Inn nor the Prince o' Wales. I suppose something you've done's set him off.

MRS HOLROYD: It's nothing I've done.

GRANDMOTHER: Eh, if he's gone off and left you, whativer shall we do! Whativer 'ave you been doing?

MRS HOLROYD: He brought a couple of bright daisies here last night—two of those trollops from Nottingham—and I said I'd not have it.

GRANDMOTHER (*sighing deeply*): Ay, you've never been able to agree.

MRS HOLROYD: We agreed well enough except when he drank like a fish and came home rolling.

GRANDMOTHER (*whining*): Well, what can you expect of a man as 'as been shut up i' th' pit all day? He must have a bit of relaxation.

MRS HOLROYD: He can have it different from that, then. At any rate, I'm sick of it.

GRANDMOTHER: Ay, you've a stiff neck, but it'll be bowed by you're my age.

MRS HOLROYD: Will it? I'd rather it were broke.

GRANDMOTHER: Well—there's no telling what a jealous man will do. (*She shakes her head.*)

MRS HOLROYD: Nay, I think it's my place to be jealous, when he brings a brazen hussy here and sits carryin' on with her.

GRANDMOTHER: He'd no business to do that. But you know, Lizzie, he's got something on *his* side.

MRS HOLROYD: What, pray?

GRANDMOTHER: Well, I don't want to make any mischief, but you're my son's wife, an' it's nothing but my duty to tell you. They've been saying a long time now as that young electrician is here a bit too often.

MRS HOLROYD: He doesn't come for my asking.

GRANDMOTHER: No, I don't suppose he wants for asking. But Charlie's not the man to put up with that sort o' work.

MRS HOLROYD: Charlie put up with it! If he's anything to say, why doesn't he say it, without going to other folks . . . ?

GRANDMOTHER: Charlie's never been near me with a word —nor 'as he said a word elsewhere to my knowledge. For all that, this is going to end with trouble.

MRS HOLROYD: In this hole, every gossiping creature thinks she's got the right to cackle about you—sickening! And a parcel of lies.

GRANDMOTHER: Well, Lizzie, I've never said anything against you. Charlie's been a handful of trouble. He made my heart ache once or twice afore you had him, and he's made it ache many, many's the time since. But it's not all on his side, you know.

MRS HOLROYD (*hotly*): No, I don't know.

GRANDMOTHER: You thought yourself above him, Lizzie, an' you know he's not the man to stand it.

MRS HOLROYD: No, he's run away from it.

GRANDMOTHER (*venomously*): And what man wouldn't leave a woman that allowed him to live on sufferance in the house with her, when he was bringing the money home?

MRS HOLROYD: 'Sufferance!'—Yes, there's been a lot of letting him live on 'sufferance' in the house with me. It is *I* who have lived on sufferance, for his service and pleasure. No, what he wanted was the drink and the public house company, and because he couldn't get them here, he went out for them. That's all.

GRANDMOTHER: You have always been very clever at hitting things off, Lizzie. I was always sorry my youngest son married a clever woman. He only wanted a bit of coaxing and managing, and you clever women won't do it.

MRS HOLROYD: He wanted a slave, not a wife.

GRANDMOTHER: It's a pity your stomach wasn't too high for him, before you had him. But no, you could have eaten him ravishing at one time.

MRS HOLROYD: It's a pity you didn't tell me what he was before I had him. But no, he was all angel. You left me to find out what he really was.

GRANDMOTHER: Some women could have lived with him happy enough. An' a fat lot you'd have thanked me for my telling.

There is a knock at the door, MRS HOLROYD *opens.*

RIGLEY: They tell me, missus, as your mester's not hoom yet.

MRS HOLROYD: No—who is it?

GRANDMOTHER: Ask him to step inside. Don't stan' there lettin' the fog in.

RIGLEY *steps in. He is a tall, bony, very roughly hewn collier.*

RIGLEY: Good evenin'.

GRANDMOTHER: Oh, is it you, Mr Rigley? (*In a querulous, spiteful tone to* MRS HOLROYD.) He butties along with Charlie.

MRS HOLROYD: Oh!

RIGLEY: Au' han yer seen nowt on 'im?

MRS HOLROYD: No—was he all right at work?

RIGLEY: Well, e' wor nowt to mention. A bit short, like: 'adna much to say, I canna ma'e out what 'e's done wi' 'issen. (*He is manifestly uneasy, does not look at the two women.*)

GRANDMOTHER: An' did 'e come up i' th' same bantle wi' you?

RIGLEY: No—'e didna. As Ah was comin' out o' th' stall, Ah shouted, 'Art comin', Charlie? We're a' off.' An' 'e said, 'Ah'm comin' in a minute.' 'E wor just finishin' a stint, like, an' 'e wanted ter get it set. An' 'e 'd been a bit roughish in 'is temper, like, so I thöwt 'e didna want ter walk to th' bottom wi' us. . . .

GRANDMOTHER (*wailing*): An' what's 'e gone an' done to himself?

RIGLEY: Nay, missis, yo munna ax me that. 'E's non done owt as Ah know on. On'y I wor thinkin', 'appen summat 'ad 'appened to 'im, like, seein' as nob'dy had any knowings of 'im comin' up.

MRS HOLROYD: What is the matter, Mr Rigley? Tell us it out.

RIGLEY: I canna do that, missis. It seems as if 'e niver come up th' pit—as far as we can make out. 'Appen a bit o' stuff's fell an' pinned 'im.

GRANDMOTHER (*wailing*): An' 'ave you left 'im lying down there in the pit, poor thing?

RIGLEY (*uneasily*): I couldna say for certain where 'e is.

MRS HOLROYD (*agitated*): Oh, it's very likely not very bad, mother! Don't let us run to meet trouble.

RIGLEY: We 'ave to 'ope for th' best, missis, all on us.

GRANDMOTHER (*wailing*): Eh, they'll bring 'im 'ome, I know they will, smashed up an' broke! An' one of my sons they've burned down pit till the flesh dropped off 'im, an' one was shot till 'is shoulder was all of a mosh, an' they brought 'em 'ome to me. An' now there's this. . . .

MRS HOLROYD (*shuddering*): Oh, don't, mother. (*Appealing to* RIGLEY.) You don't know that he's hurt?

RIGLEY (*shaking his head*): I canna tell you.

MRS HOLROYD (*in a high hysterical voice*): Then what is it?

RIGLEY (*very uneasy*): I canna tell you. But yon young electrician—Mr Blackmore—'e rung down to the night deputy, an' it seems as though there's been a fall or summat. . . .

GRANDMOTHER: Eh, Lizzie, you parted from him in anger. You little knowed how you'd meet him again.

RIGLEY (*making an effort*): Well, I'd 'appen best be goin' to see what's betide.

He goes out.

GRANDMOTHER: I'm sure I've had my share of bad luck, I have. I'm sure I've brought up five lads in the pit, through accidents and troubles, and now there's this. The Lord has treated me very hard, very hard. It's a blessing, Lizzie, as you've got a bit of money, else what would 'ave become of the children?

MRS HOLROYD: Well, if he's badly hurt, there'll be the Union-pay, and sick-pay—we shall manage. And perhaps perhaps it's *not* very much.

GRANDMOTHER: There's no knowin' but what they'll be carryin' him to die 'i th' hospital.

MRS HOLROYD: Oh, don't say so. mother—it won't be so bad, you'll see.

GRANDMOTHER: How much money have you. Lizzie. comin'?

MRS HOLROYD: I don't know—not much over a hundred pounds.

GRANDMOTHER (*shaking her head*): An' what's that, what's that?

MRS HOLROYD (*sharply*): Hush!

GRANDMOTHER (*crying*): Why, what?

    MRS HOLROYD *opens the door. In the silence can be heard the pulsing of the fan engine, then the driving engine chuffs rapidly: there is a skirr of brakes on the rope as it descends*

MRS HOLROYD: That's twice they've sent the chair down— I wish we could see. . . . Hark!

GRANDMOTHER: What is it?

MRS HOLROYD: Yes—it's stopped at the gate. It's the doctor's.

GRANDMOTHER (*coming to the door*): What, Lizzie?

MRS HOLROYD: The doctor's motor. (*She listens acutely.*) Dare you stop here, mother, while I run up to the top an' see?

GRANDMOTHER: You'd better not go, Lizzie, you'd better not. A woman's best away.

MRS HOLROYD: It is unbearable to wait.

GRANDMOTHER: Come in an' shut the door—it's a cold that gets in your bones.

    MRS HOLROYD *goes in.*

MRS HOLROYD: Perhaps while he's in bed we shall have time to change him. It's an ill wind brings no good. He'll happen be a better man.

GRANDMOTHER: Well, you can but try. Many a woman's thought the same.

MRS HOLROYD: Oh, dear, I wish somebody would come. He's never been hurt since we were married.

GRANDMOTHER: No, he's never had a bad accident, all the years he's been in the pit. He's been luckier than most. But everybody has it, sooner or later.

MRS HOLROYD (*shivering*): It *is* a horrid night.

GRANDMOTHER (*querulous*): Yes, come your ways in.

MRS HOLROYD: Hark!

There is a quick sound of footsteps. BLACKMORE *comes into the light of the doorway.*

BLACKMORE: They're bringing him.

MRS HOLROYD (*quickly putting her hand over her breast*): What is it?

BLACKMORE: You can't tell anything's the matter with him —it's not marked him at all.

MRS HOLROYD: Oh, what a blessing! And is it much?

BLACKMORE: Well——

MRS HOLROYD: What is it?

BLACKMORE: It's the worst.

GRANDMOTHER: Who is it?—What does he say?

MRS HOLROYD *sinks on the nearest chair with a horrified expression.* BLACKMORE *pulls himself together and enters the room. He is very pale.*

BLACKMORE: I came to tell you they're bringing him home.

GRANDMOTHER: And you said it wasn't very bad, did you?

BLACKMORE: No—I said it was—as bad as it could be.

MRS HOLROYD (*rising and crossing to her* MOTHER-IN-LAW, *flings her arms round her; in a high voice*): Oh, mother, what shall we do? What shall we do?

GRANDMOTHER: You don't mean to say he's dead?

BLACKMORE: Yes

GRANDMOTHER (*staring*): God help us, and how was it?

BLACKMORE: Some stuff fell.

GRANDMOTHER (*rocking herself and her daughter-in-law—both weeping*): Oh, God have mercy on us! Oh, God have mercy on us! Some stuff fell on him. An' he'd not even time to cry for mercy; oh, God spare him! Oh, what shall we do for comfort? To be taken straight out of his sins. Oh, Lizzie, to think he should be cut off in his wickedness. He's been a bad lad of late, he has, poor lamb. He's gone very wrong of late years, poor dear lamb, very wrong. Oh, Lizzie, think what's become of him now! If only you'd tried to be different with him.

MRS HOLROYD (*moaning*): Don't, mother, don't. I can't bear it.

BLACKMORE (*cold and clear*): Where will you have him laid? The men will be here in a moment.

MRS HOLROYD (*staring up*): They can carry him up to bed——

BLACKMORE: It's no good taking him upstairs. You'll have to wash him and lay him out.

MRS HOLROYD (*startled*): Well——

BLACKMORE: He's in his pit-dirt.

GRANDMOTHER: He is, bless him. We'd better have him down here, Lizzie, where we can handle him.

MRS HOLROYD: Yes.

She begins to put the tea things away, but drops the sugar out of the basin and the lumps fly broadcast.

BLACKMORE: Never mind, I'll pick those up. You put the children's clothes away.

MRS HOLROYD *stares witless around. The* GRAND-MOTHER *sits rocking herself and weeping.* BLACKMORE *clears the table, putting the pots in the scullery. He folds the white tablecloth and pulls back the table. The door opens,* MRS HOLROYD *utters a cry.* RIGLEY *enters.*

RIGLEY: They're bringing him now, missis.

MRS HOLROYD: Oh!

RIGLEY (*simply*): There must ha' been a fall directly after we left him.

MRS HOLROYD (*frowning, horrified*): No—no!

RIGLEY (*to* BLACKMORE): It fell a' back of him, an' shut 'im in as you might shut a loaf 'i th' oven. It never touched him.

MRS HOLROYD (*staring distractedly*): Well, then——

RIGLEY: You see, it come on 'im as close as a trap on a mouse, an' gen him no air, an' what wi' th' gas, it smothered him. An' it wouldna be so very long about it neither.

MRS HOLROYD (*quiet with horror*): Oh!

GRANDMOTHER: Eh, dear—dear. Eh, dear—dear.

RIGLEY (*looking hard at her*): I wasna to know what 'ud happen.

GRANDMOTHER (*not heeding him, but weeping all the time*): But the Lord gave him time to repent. He'd have a few minutes to repent. Ay, I hope he did, I hope he did, else what was to become of him. The Lord cut him off in his sins, but He gave him time to repent.

RIGLEY *looks away at the wall.* BLACKMORE *has made a space in the middle of the floor.*

BLACKMORE: If you'll take the rocking-chair off the end of the rug, Mrs Holroyd, I can pull it back a bit from the fire, and we can lay him on that.

GRANDMOTHER (*petulantly*): What's the good of messing about—— (*She moves.*)

MRS HOLROYD: It suffocated him?

RIGLEY (*shaking his head, briefly*): Yes. 'Appened th' after-damp——

BLACKMORE: He'd be dead in a few minutes.

MRS HOLROYD: No—oh, think!

BLACKMORE: You mustn't think.

RIGLEY (*suddenly*): They commin'!

MRS HOLROYD *stands at bay. The* GRANDMOTHER *half rises.* RIGLEY *and* BLACKMORE *efface themselves as much as possible. A man backs into the room, bearing the feet of the dead man, which are shod in great pit boots. As the head bearer comes awkwardly past the table, the coat with which the body is covered slips off, revealing* HOLROYD *in his pit-dirt, naked to the waist.*

MANAGER (*a little stout, white-bearded man*): Mind now, mind.

Ay, missis, what a job, indeed, it is! (*Sharply.*) Where mun they put him?

MRS HOLROYD (*turning her face aside from the corpse*): Lay him on the rug.

MANAGER: Steady now, do it steady.

SECOND BEARER (*rising and pressing back his shoulders*): By Guy, but 'e 'ings heavy.

MANAGER: Yi, Joe, I'll back my life o' that.

GRANDMOTHER: Eh, Mr Chambers, what's this affliction on my old age. You kept your sons out o' the pit, but all mine's in. And to think of the trouble I've had—to think o' the trouble that's come out of Brinsley pit to me.

MANAGER: It has that, it 'as that, missis. You seem to have had more'n your share; I'll admit it, you have.

MRS HOLROYD (*who has been staring at the men*): It is too much!

     BLACKMORE *frowns;* RIGLEY *glowers at her.*

MANAGER: You never knowed such a thing in your life. Here's a man, holin' a stint, just finishin', (*He puts himself as if in the holer's position, gesticulating freely.*) an' a lot o' stuff falls behind him, clean as a whistle, shuts him up safe as a worm in a nut and niver touches him—niver knowed such a thing in your life.

MRS HOLROYD: Ugh!

MANAGER: It niver hurt him—niver touched him.

MRS HOLROYD: Yes, but—but how long would he be (*She makes a sweeping gesture; the* MANAGER *looks at her and will not help her out.*)—how long would it take—ah—to—to kill him?

MANAGER: Nay, I canna tell ye. 'E didna seem to ha' strived much to get out—did he, Joe?

SECOND BEARER: No, not as far as Ah'n seen.

FIRST BEARER: You look at 'is 'ands, you'll see then. 'E'd non ha'e room to swing the pick.

     The MANAGER *goes on his knees.*

MRS HOLROYD (*shuddering*): Oh, don't!

MANAGER: Ay, th' nails is broken a bit——

MRS HOLROYD (*clenching her fists*): Don't!

MANAGER: 'E'd be sure ter ma'e a bit of a fight. But th' gas 'ud soon get hold on 'im. Ay, it's an awful thing to think of, it is indeed.

MRS HOLROYD (*her voice breaking*): I can't bear it!

MANAGER: Eh, dear, we none on us know what's comin' next.

MRS HOLROYD (*getting hysterical*): Oh, it's too awful, it's too awful!

BLACKMORE: You'll disturb the children.

GRANDMOTHER: And you don't want *them* down here.

MANAGER: 'E'd no business to ha' been left, you know.

RIGLEY: An' what man, dost think, wor goin' to sit him down on his hams an' wait for a chap as wouldna say 'thank yer' for his cump'ny? 'E'd bin ready to fall out wi' a flicker o' the candle, so who dost think wor goin' ter stop when we knowed 'e on'y kep on so's to get shut on us.

MANAGER: Tha'rt quite right, Bill, quite right. But theer you are.

RIGLEY: Ah' if we'd stopped, what good would it ha' done——

MANAGER: No, 'appen not, 'appen not.

RIGLEY: For, not known——

MANAGER: I'm sayin' nowt agen thee, neither one road nor t'other. (*There is a general silence—then, to* MRS HOLROYD.) I should think th' inquest'll be at th' New Inn to-morrow, missis. I'll let you know.

MRS HOLROYD: Will there have to be an inquest?

MANAGER: Yes—there'll have to be an inquest. Shall you want anybody in, to stop with you to-night?

MRS HOLROYD: No.

MANAGER: Well, then, we'd best be goin'. I'll send my missis down first thing in the morning. It's a bad job, a bad job, it is. You'll be a' right then?

MRS HOLROYD: Yes.

MANAGER: Well, good night then—good night all.

ALL: Good night. Good night.

    The MANAGER, *followed by the two bearers, goes out, closing the door.*

RIGLEY: It's like this, missis. I never should ha' gone, if he hadn't wanted us to.

MRS HOLROYD: Yes, I know.

RIGLEY: 'E wanted to come up by 's sen.

MRS HOLROYD (*wearily*): I know how it was, Mr Rigley.

RIGLEY: Yes——

BLACKMORE: Nobody could foresee.

RIGLEY (*shaking his head*): No. If there's owt, missis, as you want——

MRS HOLROYD: Yes—I think there isn't anything.

RIGLEY (*after a moment*): Well—good night—we've worked i' the same stall ower four years now——

MRS HOLROYD: Yes.

RIGLEY: Well, good night, missis.

MRS HOLROYD AND BLACKMORE: Good night.

    The GRANDMOTHER *all this time has been rocking herself to and fro, moaning and murmuring beside the dead man. When* RIGLEY *has gone* MRS HOLROYD *stands staring distractedly before her. She has not yet looked at her husband.*

GRANDMOTHER: Have you got the things ready, Lizzie?

MRS HOLROYD: What things?

GRANDMOTHER: To lay the child out.

MRS HOLROYD (*she shudders*): No—what?

GRANDMOTHER: Haven't you put him by a pair o' white stockings, nor a white shirt?

MRS HOLROYD: He's got a white cricketing shirt—but not white stockings.

GRANDMOTHER: Then he'll have to have his father's. Let me look at the shirt, Lizzie. (MRS HOLROYD *takes one from the dresser drawer.*) This'll never do—a cold, canvas thing wi' a turndown collar. I s'll 'ave to fetch his father's. (*Suddenly.*) You don't want no other woman to touch him, to wash him and lay him out, do you?

MRS HOLROYD (*weeping*): No.

GRANDMOTHER: Then I'll fetch him his father's gear. We mustn't let him set, he'll be that heavy, bless him. (*She takes her shawl.*) I shan't be more than a few minutes, an' the young fellow can stop here till I come back.

BLACKMORE: Can't I go for you, Mrs Holroyd?

GRANDMOTHER: No. *You* couldn't find the things. We'll wash him as soon as I get back, Lizzie.

MRS HOLROYD: All right.

She watches her mother-in-law go out. Then she starts, goes in the scullery for a bowl, in which she pours warm water. She takes a flannel and soap and towel. She stands, afraid to go any further.

BLACKMORE: Well!

MRS HOLROYD: This is a judgment on us.

BLACKMORE: Why?

MRS HOLROYD: On me, it is——

BLACKMORE: How?

MRS HOLROYD: It is.

BLACKMORE *shakes his head.*

MRS HOLROYD: Yesterday, you talked of murdering him.

BLACKMORE: Well!

MRS HOLROYD: Now we've done it.

BLACKMORE: How?

MRS HOLROYD: He'd have come up with the others, if he hadn't felt—felt me murdering him.

BLACKMORE: But we can't help it.

MRS HOLROYD: It's my fault.

BLACKMORE: Don't be like that!

MRS HOLROYD (*looking at him—then indicating her husband*): I daren't see him.

BLACKMORE: No?

MRS HOLROYD: I've killed him, that is all.

BLACKMORE: No, you haven't.

MRS HOLROYD: Yes, I have.

BLACKMORE: *We* couldn't help it.

MRS HOLROYD: If he hadn't felt, if he hadn't *known*, he wouldn't have stayed, he'd have come up with the rest.

BLACKMORE: Well, and even if it was so, we can't help it now.

MRS HOLROYD: But we've killed him.

BLACKMORE: Ah, I'm tired——

MRS HOLROYD: Yes.

BLACKMORE (*after a pause*): Shall I stay?

MRS HOLROYD: I—I daren't be alone with him.

BLACKMORE (*sitting down*): No.

MRS HOLROYD: I don't love him. Now he's dead. I don't love him. He lies like he did yesterday.

BLACKMORE: I suppose, being dead—I don't know——

MRS HOLROYD: I think you'd better go.

BLACKMORE (*rising*): Tell me.

MRS HOLROYD: Yes.

BLACKMORE: You want me to go.

MRS HOLROYD: No—but *do* go. (*They look at each other.*)

BLACKMORE I shall come to-morrow.

   BLACKMORE *goes out.*

   MRS HOLROYD *stands very stiff, as if afraid of the dead man. Then she stoops down and begins to sponge his face, talking to him.*

MRS HOLROYD: My dear, my dear—oh, my dear! I can't bear it, my dear—you shouldn't have done it. You shouldn't have done it. Oh—I can't bear it, for you. Why couldn't I do anything for you? The children's father—my dear— I wasn't good to you. But you shouldn't have done this to me. Oh, dear, oh, dear! Did it hurt you!—oh, my dear, it hurt you—oh, I can't bear it. No, things aren't fair—we went wrong, my dear. I never loved you enough—I never

did. What a shame for you! It was a shame. But you didn't
—you didn't try. I *would* have loved you—I tried hard.
What a shame for you! It was so cruel for you. You
couldn't help it—my dear, my dear. You couldn't help it.
And I can't do anything for you, and it hurt you so! (*She
weeps bitterly, so her tears fall on the dead man's face; suddenly
she kisses him.*) My dear, my dear, what can I do for you,
what can I? (*She weeps as she wipes his face gently.*)

    Enter GRANDMOTHER.

GRANDMOTHER (*putting a bundle on the table, and taking off
her shawl*): You're not all by yourself?

MRS HOLROYD: Yes.

GRANDMOTHER: It's a wonder you're not frightened. You've
not washed his face.

MRS HOLROYD: Why should I be afraid of him—now,
mother?

GRANDMOTHER (*weeping*): Ay, poor lamb, I can't think as
ever you could have had reason to be frightened of him,
Lizzie.

MRS HOLROYD: Yes—once——

GRANDMOTHER: Oh, but he went wrong. An' he was a
taking lad, as iver was. (*She cries pitifully.*) And when I
waked his father up and told him, he sat up in bed staring
over his whiskers, and said should he come up? But when
I'd managed to find the shirt and things, he was still in bed.
You don't know what it is to live with a man that has no
feeling. But you've washed him, Lizzie?

MRS HOLROYD: I was finishing his head.

GRANDMOTHER: Let me do it, child.

MRS HOLROYD: I'll finish that.

GRANDMOTHER: Poor lamb—poor dear lamb! Yet I
wouldn't wish him back, Lizzie. He must ha' died peaceful,
Lizzie. He seems to be smiling. He always had such a rare
smile on him—not that he's smiled much of late——

MRS HOLROYD: I loved him for that.

GRANDMOTHER: Ay, my poor child—my poor child.

MRS HOLROYD: He looks nice, mother.

GRANDMOTHER: I hope he made his peace with the Lord.

MRS HOLROYD: Yes.

GRANDMOTHER: If he hadn't time to make his peace with the Lord, I've no hopes of him. Dear o' me, dear o' me. Is there another bit of flannel anywhere?

MRS HOLROYD *rises and brings a piece. The* GRANDMOTHER *begins to wash the breast of the dead man.*

GRANDMOTHER: Well, I hope you'll be true to his children at least, Lizzie. (MRS HOLROYD *weeps—the old woman continues her washing.*) Eh—and he's fair as a lily. Did you ever see a man with a whiter skin—and flesh as fine as the driven snow. He's beautiful, he is, the lamb. Many's the time I've looked at him, and I've felt proud of him, I have. And now he lies here. And such arms on 'im! Look at the vaccination marks, Lizzie. When I took him to be vaccinated, he had a little pink bonnet with a feather. (*Weeps.*) Don't cry, my girl, don't. Sit up an' wash him a' that side, or we s'll never have him done. Oh, Lizzie!

MRS HOLROYD (*sitting up, startled*): What—what?

GRANDMOTHER: Look at his poor hand!

She holds up the right hand. The nails are bloody.

MRS HOLROYD: Oh, no! Oh, no! No!

Both women weep.

GRANDMOTHER (*after a while*): We maun get on, Lizzie.

MRS HOLROYD (*sitting up*): I can't touch his hands.

GRANDMOTHER: But I'm his mother—there's nothing I couldn't do for him.

MRS HOLROYD: I don't care—I don't care.

GRANDMOTHER: Prithee, prithee, Lizzie, I don't want thee goin' off, Lizzie.

MRS HOLROYD (*moaning*): Oh, what shall I do!

GRANDMOTHER: Why, go thee an' get his feet washed. He's setting stiff, and how shall we get him laid out?

MRS HOLROYD, *sobbing, goes, kneels at the miner's feet, and begins pulling off the great boots.*

GRANDMOTHER: There's hardly a mark on him. Eh, what a man he is! I've had some fine sons, Lizzie, I've had some big men of sons.

MRS HOLROYD: He was always a lot whiter than me. And he used to chaff me.

GRANDMOTHER: But his poor hands! I used to thank God for my children, but they're rods o' trouble, Lizzie, they are. Unfasten his belt, child. We mun get his things off soon, or else we s'll have such a job.

MRS HOLROYD, *having dragged off his boots, rises. She is weeping.*

CURTAIN

The Daughter-in-Law

CHARACTERS

MRS GASCOIGNE

JOE

MRS PURDY

MINNIE

LUTHER

Act I takes place in Mrs Gascoigne's kitchen, and Acts II, III and IV in the kitchen of Luther Gascoigne's new home

ACT ONE

SCENE ONE

*A collier's kitchen—not poor. Windsor chairs, deal table, dresser of
painted wood, sofa covered with red cotton stuff. Time: About
half-past two of a winter's afternoon.*

*A large, stoutish woman of sixty-five, with smooth black hair
parted down the middle of her head:* MRS GASCOIGNE.

*Enter a young man, about twenty-six, dark, good-looking; has his
right arm in a sling; does not take off cap:* JOE GASCOIGNE.

MRS GASCOIGNE: Well, I s'd ha' thought thy belly 'ud a
brow't thee whoam afore this.

    JOE *sits on sofa without answering.*

Doesn't ter want no dinner?

JOE (*looking up*): I want it if the' is ony.

MRS GASCOIGNE: An' if the' isna, tha can go be out? Tha
talks large, my fine jockey! (*She puts a newspaper on the
table; on it a plate and his dinner.*) Wheer dost reckon ter's
bin?

JOE: I've bin ter th' office for my munny.

MRS GASCOIGNE: Tha's niver bin a' this while at th' office.

JOE: They kep' me ower an hour, an' then gen me nowt.

MRS GASCOIGNE: Gen thee nowt! Why, how do they ma'e
that out? It's a wik sin' tha got hurt, an' if a man wi' a
broken arm canna ha' his fourteen shillin' a week accident
pay, who can, I s'd like to know?

JOE: They'll gie me nowt, whether or not.

MRS GASCOIGNE: An' for why, prithee?

JOE (*does not answer for some time; then, sullenly*): They reckon
I niver got it while I wor at work.

MRS GASCOIGNE: Then where did ter get it, might I ax? I'd think they'd like to lay it onto me.

JOE: Tha talks like a fool, Mother.

MRS GASCOIGNE: Tha looks like one, me lad.

She has given him his dinner; he begins to eat with a fork.
Here, hutch up, gammy-leg—gammy-arm.

He makes room; she sits by him on the sofa and cuts up his meat for him.
It's a rum un as I should start ha'in' babies again, an' feedin' 'em wi' spoon-meat. (*Gives him a spoon.*) An' now let's hear why they winna gi'e thee thy pay. Another o' Macintyre's dirty knivey dodges, I s'd think.

JOE: They reckon I did it wi' foolery, an' not wi' work.

MRS GASCOIGNE: Oh indeed! An' what by that?

JOE (*eating*): They wunna gie me nowt, that's a'.

MRS GASCOIGNE: It's a nice thing! An' what did ter say?

JOE: I said nowt.

MRS GASCOIGNE: Tha wouldna'! Tha stood like a stuffed duck, an' said thank-yer.

JOE: Well, it wor raight.

MRS GASCOIGNE: How raight?

JOE: I did do it wi' foolery.

MRS GASCOIGNE: Then what did ter go axin' fer pay fer?

JOE: I did it at work, didna I? An' a man as gets accident at work's titled ter disability-pay, isna he?

MRS GASCOIGNE: Tha said a minnit sin' as tha got it wi' foolery.

JOE: An' so I did.

MRS GASCOIGNE: I niver 'eered such talk i' my life.

JOE: I dunna care what ter's 'eered an' what t'asna. I wor foolin' wi' a wringer an' a pick-heft—ta's it as ter's a mind.

MRS GASCOIGNE: What, down pit?

JOE: I' th' stall, at snap-time.

MRS GASCOIGNE: Showin' off a bit, like?

JOE: Ye'.

MRS GASCOIGNE: An' what then?

JOE: Th' wringer gen me a rap ower th'arm, an' that's a'.

MRS GASCOIGNE: An' tha reported it as a accident?

JOE: It wor accident, worn't it? I niver did it a'purpose.

MRS GASCOIGNE: But a pit accident.

JOE: Well, an' what else wor't? It wor a h'accident I got i' th' pit, i' th' sta' wheer I wor workin'.

MRS GASCOIGNE: But not *while* tha wor workin'.

JOE: What by that?—it wor a pit accident as I got i' th' stall.

MRS GASCOIGNE: But tha didna tell 'em how it happened.

JOE: I said some stuff fell on my arm, an' brok' it. An' worna that trew?

MRS GASCOIGNE: It wor very likely trew enough, lad, if on'y they'd ha' believed it.

JOE: An they would ha' believed it, but for Hewett bully-raggin' Bettesworth 'cos he knowed he was a chappil man. (*He imitates the underground manager, Hewett, and Bettesworth, a butty.*) 'About this accident, Bettesworth. How exactly did it occur?' 'I couldn't exactly say for certing, sir, because I wasn't linkin'.' 'Then tell me as near as you can.' 'Well, Mester, I'm sure I don't know.' 'That's curious, Bettesworth—I must have a report. Do you know anything about it, or don't you? It happened in your stall; you're responsible for it, and I'm responsible for you.' 'Well, Gaffer, what's right's right, I suppose, ter th' mesters or th' men. An' e' wor conjurin' a' snap-time wi' a pick-heft an' a wringer, an' the wringer catched 'im ower th' arm.' 'I thought you didn't know!' 'I said *for certain*—I didn't see exactly how 'twas done.'

MRS GASCOIGNE: Hm.

JOE: Bettesworth 'ud non ha' clat-fasted but for nosy Hewett. He says, 'Yo know, Joseph, when he says to me, "Do you know anything about that haccident?"—then I says to myself, "Take not the word of truth hutterly outer thy mouth."'

MRS GASCOIGNE: If he took a bit o' slaver outen's mouth, it 'ud do.

JOE: So this mornin' when I went ter th' office, Mester Salmon he com out an' said: "Ow did this haccident occur, Joseph?' and I said, 'Some stuff fell on't.' So he says, 'Stuff fell on't, stuff fell on't! You mean coal or rock or what?' So I says, 'Well, it worn't a thipenny bit.' 'No,' he says, 'but what was it?' 'It wor a piece o' clunch,' I says. 'You don't use clunch for wringers,' he says, 'do you?' 'The wringin' of the nose bringeth forth blood,' I says——

MRS GASCOIGNE: Why, you know you never did. (*She begins making a pudding.*)

JOE: No—b'r I'd ha' meant t'r'a done.

MRS GASCOIGNE: We know thee! Tha's done thysen one i' th' eye this time. When dost think tha'll iver get ter be a butty, at this rate? There's Luther nowt b'r a day man yet.

JOE: I'd as lief be a day man as a butty, i' pits that rat-gnawed there's hardly a stall worth havin'; an' a company as 'ud like yer ter scrape yer tabs afore you went home, for fear you took a grain o' coal.

MRS GASCOIGNE: Maybe—but tha's got ter get thy livin' by 'em.

JOE: I hanna. I s'll go to Australia.

MRS GASCOIGNE: Tha'lt do no such thing, while I'm o' this earth.

JOE: Ah, but though, I shall—else get married, like our Luther.

MRS GASCOIGNE: A fat sight better off tha'lt be for that.

JOE: You niver know, Mother, dun yer?

MRS GASCOIGNE: You dunna, me lad—not till yer find yerself let in. Marriage is like a mouse-trap, for either man or woman. You've soon come to th' end o' th' cheese.

JOE: Well, ha'ef a loaf's better nor no bread.

MRS GASCOIGNE: Why, wheer's th' loaf as tha'd like ter gnawg a' thy life?

JOE: Nay, nowhere yet.

MRS GASCOIGNE: Well, dunna thee talk, then. Tha's done thysen harm enow for one day, wi' thy tongue.

JOE: An' good as well, Mother—I've aten my dinner, a'most.

MRS GASCOIGNE: An' swilled thy belly afore that, methinks.

JOE: Niver i' this world!

MRS GASCOIGNE: And I've got thee to keep on ten shillin's a wik club-money, han I?

JOE: Tha needna, if ter doesna want. Besides, we s'll be out on strike afore we know wheer we are.

MRS GASCOIGNE: I'm sure. You've on'y bin in——

JOE: Now, Mother, spit on thy hands an' ta'e fresh hold. We s'll be out on strike in a wik or a fortnit——

MRS GASCOIGNE: Strike's a' they're fit for—a pack o' slutherers as . . .

Her words tail off as she goes into pantry.

JOE (*to himself*): Tha goes chunterin' i' th' pantry when somebody's at th' door. (*Rises, goes to door.*)

MRS PURDY'S VOICE: Is your mother in?

JOE: Yi, 'er's in right enough.

MRS PURDY: Well, then, can I speak to her?

JOE (*calling*): Mrs Purdy wants ter speak to thee, Mother.

MRS GASCOIGNE *crosses the kitchen heavily, with a dripping-pan; stands in doorway.*

MRS GASCOIGNE: Good afternoon.

MRS PURDY: Good afternoon.

MRS GASCOIGNE: Er—what is it?

MRS PURDY *enters. She is a little fat, red-faced body in bonnet and black cape.*

MRS PURDY: I wanted to speak to yer rather pertickler.

MRS GASCOIGNE (*giving way*): Oh, yes?

ALL THREE *enter the kitchen.* MRS PURDY *stands near the door.*

MRS PURDY (*nodding to* JOE): Has he had a haccident?

MRS GASCOIGNE: Broke his arm.

MRS PURDY: Oh my! that's nasty. When did 'e do that?

MRS GASCOIGNE: A wik sin' to-day.

MRS PURDY: In th' pit?

MRS GASCOIGNE: Yes—an's not goin' to get any accident pay—says as 'e worn't workin'; he wor foolin' about.

MRS PURDY: T-t-t-t! Did iver you know! I tell you what, missis, it's a wonder they let us live on the face o' the earth at all—it's a wonder we don't have to fly up i' th' air like birds.

JOE: There'd be a squark i' th' sky then!

MRS PURDY: But it is indeed. It's somethink awful. They've gave my mester a dirty job o' nights, at a guinea a week, an' he's worked fifty years for th' company, an' isn't but sixty-two now—said he wasn't equal to stall-workin', whereas he has to slave on th' roads an' comes whoam that tired he can't put's food in's mouth.

JOE: He's about like me.

MRS PURDY: Yis. But it's no nice thing, a guinea a week.

MRS GASCOIGNE: Well, that's how they're servin' 'em a' round—widders' coals stopped—leadin' raised to four-an'-eight—an' ivry man niggled down to nothink.

MRS PURDY: I wish I'd got that Fraser strung up by th' heels —I'd ma'e *his* sides o' bacon rowdy.

MRS GASCOIGNE: He's put a new manager to ivry pit, an' ivry one a slave-driver.

MRS PURDY: Says he's got to economise—says the company's not a philanthropic concern——

MRS GASCOIGNE: But ta'es twelve hundred a year for hissen.

MRS PURDY: A mangy bachelor wi' 'is iron-men.

JOE: But they wunna work.

MRS PURDY: They say how he did but coss an' swear about them American Cutters. I should like to see one set outer 'im—they'd work hard enough rippin's guts out—even iron's got enough sense for that. (*She suddenly subsides.*)

    There is a pause.

MRS GASCOIGNE: How do you like living down Nether-green?

MRS PURDY: Well—we're very comfortable. It's small, but it's handy, an' sin' the mester's gone down t'a guinea——

MRS GASCOIGNE: It'll do for you three.

MRS PURDY: Yes.

Another pause.

MRS GASCOIGNE: The men are comin' out again, they say.

MRS PURDY: Isn't it summat sickenin'? Well, I've werritted an' werritted till I'm soul-sick——

JOE: It sends yer that thin an' threadbare, y'have ter stop sometime.

MRS PURDY: There can be as much ache in a motherly body as in bones an' gristle, I'm sure o' that.

JOE: Nay, I'm more than bones an' gristle.

MRS PURDY: That's true as the day.

Another long pause.

MRS GASCOIGNE: An' how have yer all bin keepin'?

MRS PURDY: Oh, very nicely—except our Bertha.

MRS GASCOIGNE: Is she poorly, then?

MRS PURDY: That's what I com ter tell yer. I niver knowed a word on't till a Sat'day, nor niver noticed a thing. Then she says to me, as white as a sheet, 'I've been sick every morning, Mother,' an' it com across me like a shot from a gun. I sunk down i' that chair an' couldna fetch a breath.— An' me as prided myself! I've often laughed about it, an' said I was thankful my children had all turned out so well, lads an' wenches as well, an' said it was a'cause they was all got of a Sunday—their father was too drunk a' Saturday, an' too tired o' wik-days. An' it's a fact, they've all turned out well, for I'd allers bin to chappil. Well, I've said it for a joke, but now it's turned on me. I'd better ha' kep' my tongue still.

JOE: It's not me, though, missis. I wish it wor.

MRS PURDY: There's no occasions to ma'e gam' of it neither,

as far as I can see. The youngest an' the last of 'em as I've
got, an' a lass as I liked, for she's simple, but she's good-
natured, an' him a married man. Thinks I to myself, 'I'd
better go to's mother, she'll ha'e more about 'er than's
new wife—for she's a stuck-up piece o' goods as ever
trod.'

MRS GASCOIGNE: Why, what d'yer mean?

MRS PURDY: I mean what I say—an' there's no denyin' it.
That girl—well, it's nigh on breakin' my heart, for I'm
that sort o' breath. (*Sighs.*) I'm sure!

MRS GASCOIGNE: Why don't yer say what yer mean?

MRS PURDY: I've said it, haven't I? There's my gal gone
four month wi' childt to your Luther.

MRS GASCOIGNE: Nay, nay, nay, missis! You'll never ma'e
me believe it.

MRS PURDY: Glad would I be if I nedna. But I've gone
through it all since Sat'day on. I've wanted to break every
bone in 'er body—an' I've said I should on'y be happy if I
was scraightin' at 'er funeral—an' I've said I'd wring his
neck for 'im. But it doesn't alter it—there it is—an' there
it will be. An' I s'll be a grandmother where my heart
heaves, an' maun drag a wastrel baby through my old age.
An' it's neither a cryin' nor a laughin' matter, but it's a
matter of a girl wi' child, an' a man six week married.

MRS GASCOIGNE: But our Luther never went wi' your
Bertha. How d'you make it out?

MRS PURDY: Yea, yea, missis—yea indeed.

JOE: Yi, Mother, he's bin out wi' 'er. She wor pals wi' Liza
Ann Varley, as went out wi' Jim Horrocks. So Jim he
passed Bertha onter our Luther. Why, I've had many a
glass wi' the four of 'em, i' 'Th' Ram'.

MRS GASCOIGNE: I niver knowed nowt o' *this* afore.

JOE: Tha doesna know ivrythink, Mother.

MRS GASCOIGNE: An' it's well I don't, methinks.

JOE: Tha doesna want, neither.

MRS GASCOIGNE: Well, I dunno what we're goin' to do, missis. He's a young married man.

MRS PURDY: An' she's a girl o' mine.

MRS GASCOIGNE: How old is she?

MRS PURDY: She wor twenty-three last September.

MRS GASCOIGNE: Well then, I sh'd 'a thought she'd ha' known better.

MRS PURDY: An' what about him, missis, as goes and gets married t'r another fine madam d'rectly after he's been wi' my long lass?

JOE: But he never knowed owt about.

MRS PURDY: He'd seen th' blossom i' flower, if he handna spotted the fruit a-comin'.

JOE: Yi—but——

MRS GASCOIGNE: Yi but what?

JOE: Well—you dunna expect—ivry time yer cast yer bread on th' wathers, as it'll come whoam to you like.

MRS GASCOIGNE: Well, I dunno what we're goin' to do.

MRS PURDY: I thought I'd better come to you, rather than

——

JOE: Ah, you non want it gettin' about—an' *she'd* best not know—if it can be helped.

MRS GASCOIGNE: I can't see for why.

MRS PURDY: No indeed—a man as plays fast an' loose first wi' one an' then goes an' marries another stuck-up piece . . .

MRS GASCOIGNE: An' a wench as goes sittin' i' 'Th' Ram' wi' th' fellers mun expect what she gets, missis.

MRS PURDY: 'Appen so, 'appen so. An' th' man maun abide by what he's gi'en.

MRS GASCOIGNE: I dunno *what* we're goin' to do!

JOE: We'd best keep it as quiet as we can.

MRS PURDY: I thinks to mysen, 'It'll non become *me* to go an' jack up a married couple, for if *he's* at fault, it's her as 'ud ha'e ter suffer.' An' though she's haughty, I knowed her mother, as nice a body as ever stept, an' treated scandylos by Jim Hetherington. An', thinks I, she's a horphan, if she's got money, an' nobbut her husband i' th' world. Thinks I to mysen it's no good visitin' it on 'er head, if he's a villain. For whatever th' men does, th' women maun ma'e up for. An' though I do consider as it's nowt b'r a dirty trick o' his'n to ta'e a poor lass like my long thing, an' go an' marry a woman wi' money——

MRS GASCOIGNE: Woman wi' money, an' peace go wi' 'er, 'er an' 'er money! What she's got, she'll keep, you take my word for it, missis.

MRS PURDY: Yes, an' she's right of it.

JOE: Nay, Mother, she's non close.

MRS GASCOIGNE: Isn't she?—oh, isn't she? An' what is she then? All she wanted was as much for her money as she could get. An' when she fun as nob'dy was for sale but our Luther, she says, 'Well, I'll take it.'

JOE: Nay, it worna like that—it wor him as wor that come-day-go-day——

MRS PURDY: God send Sunday.

MRS GASCOIGNE: An' what more canna man do, think yer, but ax a woman? When has *thee* ever done as much?

JOE: No, I hanna, 'cos I've niver seen th' woman as I wanted to say 'snap'—but he slormed an' she——

MRS GASCOIGNE: Slormed! Thee slorm but one fiftieth part to any lass thee likes, an' see if 'er's not all over thee afore tha's said six words. Slormed! 'Er wor that high an' mighty, 'er wanted summat bett'nor 'im.

JOE: Nay—I reckon he niver showed the spunk of a sprat-herring to 'er.

MRS GASCOIGNE: Did *thee* show any more? Hast iver done? Yet onybody 'ud think tha wor for marryin' 'er thysen.

JOE: If I'd ha' *bin* for marryin' 'er, I'd ha' gone wholesale, not ha' fudged and haffled.

MRS GASCOIGNE: But tha *worna* for marryin' neither 'er nor nobody.

JOE: No, I worna.

MRS GASCOIGNE: No, tha worna.

There is a long pause. The mother turns half apologetically, half explanatorily, to MRS PURDY.

It's like this 'ere, missis, if you'll not say nothink about it—sin' it's got to come out atween us. He courted Minnie Hetherington when she wor at her uncle's, at th' 'Bell o' Brass', an' he wor nowt bu'r a lad o' twenty-two, an' she twenty-one. An' he wor gone on 'er right enow. Then she had that row wi' 'er uncle, for she wor iver overbearin' an' chancy. Then our Luther says to me, 'I s'll ax 'er to marry me, Mother', an' I says: 'Tha pleases thysen, but ter my thinkin' tha'rt a sight too young an' doesna know thy own mind.' Howsoever, much notice 'e takes o' me.

JOE: He took a lot o' notice on thee, tha knows well enough.

MRS GASCOIGNE: An' for what shouldn't he? Hadn't I bin a good mother to 'im i' ivry shape an' form? Let *her* make him as good a wife as I made him a mother! Well—we'll see. You'll see *him* repent the day. But they're not to be bidden. An' so, missis, he did ax 'er, as 'e'd said 'e should. But hoity-toity an' no thank yer, she wasna for havin' him, but mun go an' be a nursery governess up i' Manchester. Thinks I to myself, she's after a town johnny, a Bertie-Willie an' a yard o' cuffs. But he kep' on writin' to 'er, now an' again—an' she answered—as if she wor standin' at top of a flight of steps——

JOE: An' 'appen on'y wanted fetchin' down.

MRS GASCOIGNE: Wi' a kick from behint, if I'd ha' had th' doin' o't. So they go mornin' on' He sees 'er once i' a blew moon. If he goes ter Manchester, she condescends to see him for a couple of hours. If she comes here, she ca's i' this house wi' a 'how-do-you-do, Mrs Gascoigne', an' off again. If they go f'r a walk . . .

JOE: He's whoam again at nine o'clock.

MRS GASCOIGNE: If they go for a walk it's 'Thank you, I mustn't be very late. Good night, Luther.' I thought it 'ud niver come ter nothink. Then 'er uncle dies an' leaves her a hundred pounds, which considerin' th' way she'd been with 'im, was more than *I*'d ha' gen her—an' she was a bit nicer. She writes ter Luther ter come an' see 'er an' stop a couple o' days. He ta'es her to the the-etter, an's for goin' i' th' pit at a shillin', when she says: 'It's my treat, Luther, and five shillin' seats apiece, if you please.'

JOE: An' he couldna luik at th' performance, for fear as the folks was luikin' at 'im.

MRS GASCOIGNE: An' after th' the-etter, it must be supper wi' a man i' a tail-coat an' silver forks, an' she pays. 'Yes,' says I when he told me, 'that's the tricks of servants, showin' off afore decent folk.'

JOE: She could do what she liked, couldn't she?

MRS GASCOIGNE: Well, an' after that, he didna write, 'cept to say thank yer. For it put 'im in a horkard position. That wor four years ago, an' she's nobbut seen him three times sin' that. If she could but ha' snapped up somebody else, it 'ud bin good-bye to Luther——

JOE: As tha told him many a time.

MRS GASCOIGNE: As I told him many a time, for am I to sit an' see my own lad bitted an' bobbed, tasted an' spit out by a madam i' service? Then all of a suddin, three months back, come a letter: 'Dear Luther, I have been thinking it over, an' have come to the opinion that we'd better get married now, if we are goin' to. We've been dallying on all these years, and we seem to get no further. So we'd better make the plunge, if ever we're going to. Of course you will say exactly what you think. Don't agree to anything unless you want to. I only want to say that I think, if we're ever going to be married, we'd better do it without waiting any longer.' Well, missis, he got that letter when he com whoam fra work. I seed him porin' an' porin', but I says nowt. Then he ate some o's dinner, and went out. When he com in, it wor about half past ten, an' 'e wor white as a sheet. He gen me that letter, an' says: 'What's think o' that, Mother?' Well, you could ha' knocked me down wi' a feather when I'd read it. I says: 'I think it's tidy cheek, my lad.' He took it back an' puts 's pocket, an' after a bit, 'e says: 'What should ter say, Mother?' 'Tha says what's a mind, my lad,' I says. So he begins unlacin' 's boots. Sudden he stops, an' wi's boot-tags rattlin', goes rummagin' for th' pen an' ink. 'What art goin' to say?' I says. 'I'm goin' ter say, 'er can do as 'er's a mind. If 'er wants ter be married, 'er can, an' if 'er doesna, 'er nedna.' So I thinks we could leave it at that. He sits him down, an' doesna write more nor a side an' a haef. I thinks: 'That's done it, it'll be an end between them two now.' He niver gen th' letter to me to read.

JOE: He did to me. He says: 'I'm ready an' willin' to do what you want, whenever yer want. I'm earnin' about thirty-five bob a week, an' haven't got any money because my mother gi'es me what I ax for ter spend. But I can have what I ask for to set up house with. Your loving—Luther.' He says to me: 'Dost think it's a'right?' I says: 'I s'd think so; 'er maun ma'e what 'er likes out on't.'

MRS GASCOIGNE: On th' Monday after, she wor here livin' at 'er A'nt's an' th' notice was in at th' registrar. I says: 'What money dost want?' He says: 'Thee buy what tha thinks we s'll want.' So he tells Minnie, an' she says: 'Not bi-out I'm theer.' Well, we goes ter Nottingham, an' she will ha'e nowt b'r old-fashioned stuff. I says: 'That's niver *my* mind, Minnie.' She says: 'Well, I like it, an' yo'll see it'll look nice. I'll pay for it.' Which to be sure I never let her. For she'd had a mester as made a fool of her, tellin' her this an' that, what wor good taste, what wor bad.

JOE: An' it *does* look nice, Mother, their house.

MRS GASCOIGNE: We'll see how it looks i' ten years' time,

my lad, wi' th' racket an' tacket o' children. For it's not serviceable, missis.

MRS PURDY (*who has been a sympathetic and exclamative listener*): Then it's no good.

MRS GASCOIGNE: An' that's how they got married.

JOE: An' he went about wi's tail atween his legs, scared outer's life.

MRS GASCOIGNE: For I said no more. If he axed me owt, I did it; if he wanted owt, I got it. But it wasn't for me to go interferin' where I wasn't wanted.

JOE: If ever I get married, Mother, I s'll go i' lodgin's six month aforehand.

MRS GASCOIGNE: Tha'd better—ter get thysen a bit case-hardened.

JOE: Yi. But I'm goin' t'r Australia.

MRS GASCOIGNE: I come withee, then.

JOE: Tha doesna.

MRS GASCOIGNE: I dunna fret—tha'lt non go.

MRS PURDY: Well, it was what I should call a bit off-hand, I must say.

MRS GASCOIGNE: You can see now how he got married, an' who's to blame.

JOE: Nay, yo' canna ma'e 'er to blame for Bertha. Liza Ann Varley's ter blame for th' lass goin' out o' nights.

MRS PURDY: An' there I thought they wor both i' Varley's—not gallivantin'.

JOE: They often was. An' Jim Horrocks is ter blame fer couplin' 'er onter our Luther, an' him an' her's ter blame for the rest. I dunno how you can lay it on Minnie. You might as well lay it on 'er if th' childt wor mine.

MRS GASCOIGNE (*sharply*): Tha'd ha'e more sense!

JOE: I'd try.

MRS GASCOIGNE: But now she's played fast an' loose wi' him—twice I *know* he axed 'er to ha'e him—now she's asked for what she's got. She's put her puddin' in her mouth, an' if she's burnt herself, serve her right.

MRS PURDY: Well, I didn't want to go to court. I thought, his mother'll be th' best one to go to——

MRS GASCOIGNE: No—you mun go to him hisself—go an' tell him i' front of her—an' if she wants anythink, she mun ma'e arrangements herself.

JOE: What was you thinkin' of, Missis Purdy?

MRS PURDY: Well, I was thinkin', she's a poor lass—an' I didn't want 'er to go to court, for they ax such questions— an' I thought it was such a *thing*, him six wik married— though to be sure I'd no notions of how it was—I thought, we might happen say, it was one o' them electricians as was along when they laid th' wires under th' road down to Batsford—and——

JOE: And arrange for a lump sum, like?

MRS PURDY: Yes—we're poor, an' she's poor—an' if she had a bit o' money of 'er own—for we should niver touch it— it might be a inducement to some other young feller— for, poor long thing, she's that simple——

MRS GASCOIGNE: Well, ter my knowledge, them as has had a childt seems to get off i' marriage better nor many as hasn't. I'm sure, there's a lot o' men likes it, if they think a woman's had a baby by another man.

MRS PURDY: That's nothing to trust by, missis; you'll say so yourself.

JOE: An' about how much do you want? Thirty pounds?

MRS PURDY: We want what's fair. I got it fra Emma Stapleton; they had forty wi' their Lucy.

JOE: Forty pound?

MRS PURDY: Yes.

MRS GASCOIGNE: Well, then, let *her* find it. She's paid for nothing but the wedding. She's got money enough, if he's none. Let *her* find it. She made the bargain, she maun stick by it. It was her dip i' th' bran-tub—if there's a mouse nips hold of her finger, she maun suck it better, for nobody axed her to dip.

MRS PURDY: You think I'd better go to him? Eh, missis, it's a nasty business. But right's right.

MRS GASCOIGNE: Right *is* right, Mrs Purdy. And you go tell him a-front of her—that's the best thing you can do. Then iverything's straight.

MRS PURDY: But for her he might ha' married our Bertha.

MRS GASCOIGNE: To be sure, to be sure.

MRS PURDY: What right had she to snatch when it pleased her?

MRS GASCOIGNE: That's what I say. If th' woman ca's for th' piper, th' woman maun pay th' tune.

MRS PURDY: Not but what——

JOE: It's a nasty business.

MRS GASCOIGNE: Nasty or not, it's hers now, not mine. He's *her* husband. 'My son's my son till he takes him a wife,' an' no longer. Now let her answer for it.

MRS PURDY: An' you think I'd better go when they're both in?

MRS GASCOIGNE: I should go to-night, atween six and seven, that's what I should do.

JOE: I never should. If I was you, I'd settle it wi'out Minnie's knowin'—it's bad enough.

MRS GASCOIGNE: What's bad enough?

JOE: Why, that.

MRS GASCOIGNE: What?

JOE: Him an' 'er—it's bad enough as it is.

MRS GASCOIGNE (*with great bitterness*): Then let it be a bit worse, let it be a bit worse. Let her have it, then; it'll do her good. Who is she, to trample eggs that another hen would sit warm? No—Mrs Purdy, *give* it her. It'll take her down a peg or two, and, my sirs, she wants it, my sirs, she needs it!

JOE (*muttering*): A fat lot o' good it'll do.

MRS GASCOIGNE: What has thee ter say, I should like to

know? Fed an' clothed an' coddled, tha art, an' not a thing tha lacks. But wait till I'm gone, my lad; tha'lt know what I've done for thee, then, tha will.

JOE: For a' that, it's no good 'er knowin'.

MRS GASCOIGNE: Isna it?—isna it? If it's not good for 'er, it's good for '*im*.

JOE: I dunna believe it.

MRS GASCOIGNE: Who asked *thee* to believe it? Tha's showed thysen a wise man *this* day, hasn't ter? Wheer should ter be terday but for me? Wheer should ter iver ha' bin? An' then *tha* sits up for to talk. It ud look better o' thee not to spit i' th' hand as holds thy bread an' butter.

JOE: Neither do I.

MRS GASCOIGNE: Doesn't ter! Tha has a bit too much chelp an' chunter. It doesna go well, my lad. Tha wor blortin' an' bletherin' down at th' office a bit sin', an' a mighty fool tha made o' thysen. How should thee like to go home wi' *thy* tale o' to-day, to Minnie, might I ax thee?

JOE: If she didna like it, she could lump it.

MRS GASCOIGNE: It 'ud be thee as 'ud lump, my lad. But what does thee know about it? 'Er's rip th' guts out on thee like a tiger, an' stan' grinnin' at thee when tha shrivelled up 'cause tha'd no inside left.

MRS PURDY: She looks it, I must admit—every bit of it.

JOE: For a' that, it's no good her knowing.

MRS GASCOIGNE: Well, I say it *is*—an' thee, tha shiftly little know-all, as blorts at one minute like a suckin' calf an' th' next blethers like a hass, dunna thee come layin' th' law down to me, for I know better. No, Mrs Purdy, it's no good comin' to me. You've a right to some compensation, an' that lass o' yours has; but let them as cooked the goose eat it, that's all. Let him arrange it hisself—an' if he does nothink, put him i' court, that's all.

MRS PURDY: He's not goin' scot-free, you may back your life o' that.

MRS GASCOIGNE: You go down to-night atween six an'
seven, an' let 'em have it straight. You know where they
live?

MRS PURDY: I' Simon Street?

MRS GASCOIGNE: About four houses up—next Holbrooks.

MRS PURDY (*rising*): Yes.

JOE: An' it'll do no good. Gie me th' money, Mother; I'll
pay it.

MRS GASCOIGNE: Tha wunna!

JOE: I've a right to th' money—I've addled it.

MRS GASCOIGNE: A' right—an' I've saved it for thee. But
tha has none on't till tha knocks me down an' ta'es it out
o' my pocket.

MRS PURDY: No—let them pay themselves. It's not thy
childt, is it?

JOE: It isna—but the money is.

MRS GASCOIGNE: We'll see.

MRS PURDY: Well, I mun get back. Thank yer, missis.

MRS GASCOIGNE: And thank *you*! I'll come down to-morrow
—at dark hour.

MRS PURDY: Thank yer.—I hope yer arm'll soon be better.

JOE: Thank yer.

MRS GASCOIGNE: I'll come down to-morrow. You'll go
to-night—atween six an' seven?

MRS PURDY: Yes—if it mun be done, it mun. He took his
own way, she took hers, now I mun take mine. Well,
good afternoon. I mun see about th' mester's dinner.

JOE: And you haven't said nothink to nobody?

MRS PURDY: I haven't—I shouldn't be flig, should I?

JOE: No—I should keep it quiet as long's you can.

MRS GASCOIGNE: There's no need for a' th' world to know—
but them as is concerned maun abide by it.

MRS PURDY: Well, good afternoon.

MRS GASCOIGNE: Good afternoon.

JOE: Good afternoon.

Exit MRS PURDY.

Well, that's a winder!

MRS GASCOIGNE: Serve her right, for tip-callin' wi'm all those years.

JOE: She niver ought to know.

MRS GASCOIGNE: I—I could fetch thee a wipe ower th' face, I could!

He sulks. She is in a rage.

SCENE TWO

The kitchen of LUTHER GASCOIGNE'S *new home.*

It is pretty—in 'cottage' style; rush-bottomed chairs, black oak-bureau, brass candlesticks, delft, etc. Green cushions in chairs. Towards five o'clock. Firelight. It is growing dark.

MINNIE GASCOIGNE *is busy about the fire: a tall, good-looking young woman, in a shirt-blouse and dark skirt, and apron. She lifts lids of saucepans, etc., hovers impatiently, looks at clock, begins to trim lamp.*

MINNIE: I wish he'd come. If I didn't want him, he'd be here half-an-hour since. But just because I've got a pudding that wants eating on the tick . . . ! He—he's *never* up to the cratch; he never is. As if the day wasn't long enough!

Sound of footsteps. She seizes a saucepan, and is rushing towards the door. The latch has clacked. LUTHER *appears in the doorway, in his pit-dirt—a collier of medium height, with fair moustache. He has a red scarf knotted round his throat, and a cap with a Union medal. The two almost collide.*

LUTHER: My word, you're on the hop!

MINNIE (*disappearing into scullery*): You *nearly* made me drop the saucepan. Why are you so late?

LUTHER: I'm non late, am I?

MINNIE: You're twenty minutes later than yesterday.

LUTHER: Oh ah, I stopped finishing a stint, an' com up wi' a'most th' last batch.

He takes a tin bottle and a dirty calico snap-bag out of his pocket, puts them on the bureau; goes into the scullery.

MINNIE'S VOICE: No!

She comes hurrying out with the saucepan. In a moment, LUTHER follows. He has taken off his coat and cap, his heavy trousers are belted round his hips, his arms are bare to above the elbow, because the pit-singlet of thick flannel is almost sleeveless.

LUTHER: Tha *art* throng!

MINNIE (*at the fire, flushed*): Yes, and everything's ready, and will be spoiled.

LUTHER: Then we'd better eat it afore I wash me.

MINNIE: No—no—it's not nice——

LUTHER: Just as ter's a mind—but there's scarce a collier in a thousand washes hissen afore he has his dinner. We niver did a-whoam.

MINNIE: But it doesn't look nice.

LUTHER: Eh, wench, tha'lt soon get used ter th' looks on me. A bit o' dirt's like a veil on my face—I shine through th' 'andsomer. What hast got? (*He peers over her range.*)

MINNIE (*waving a fork*): You're not to look.

LUTHER: It smells good.

MINNIE: Are you going to have your dinner like that?

LUTHER: Ay, lass—just for once.

He spreads a newspaper in one of the green-cushioned arm-chairs and sits down. She disappears into the scullery with a saucepan. He takes off his great pit-boots. She sets a soup-tureen on the table, and lights the lamp. He watches her face in the glow.

Tha'rt non bad-luikin' when ter's a mind.

MINNIE: *When* have I a mind?

LUTHER: Tha's allers a mind—but when ter lights th' lamp

tha'rt i' luck's way.

MINNIE: Come on, then.

He drags his chair to the table.

LUTHER: I s'll ha'e ter ha'e a newspaper afront on me, or thy cloth'll be a blackymoor. (*Begins disarranging the pots.*)

MINNIE: Oh, you *are* a nuisance! (*Jumps up.*)

LUTHER: I can put 'em a' back again.

MINNIE: I know your puttings back.

LUTHER: Tha couldna get married by thysen, could ter?—so tha'lt ha'e ter ma'e th' best on me.

MINNIE: But you're such a bother—never here at the right time—never doing the right thing——

LUTHER: An' my mouth's ter wide an' my head's ter narrow. Shalt iver ha' come ter th' end of my faults an' failin's?

MINNIE (*giving him soup*): I wish I could.

LUTHER: An' now tha'lt snap mu head off 'cos I slobber, shanna tha?

MINNIE: Then don't slobber.

LUTHER: I'll try my luck. What hast bin doin' a' day?

MINNIE: Working.

LUTHER: Has our Joe bin in?

MINNIE: No. I rather thought he might, but he hasn't.

LUTHER: You've not been up home?

MINNIE: To your mother's? No, what should I go there for?

LUTHER: Eh, I dunno what ter should go for—I thought tha 'appen might.

MINNIE: But what for?

LUTHER: Nay—I niver thowt nowt about what for.

MINNIE: Then why did you ask me?

LUTHER: I dunno. (*A pause.*)

MINNIE: Your mother can come here, can't she?

LUTHER: Ay, she can come. Tha'll be goin' up wi' me to-night—I want ter go an' see about our Joe.

MINNIE: What about him?

LUTHER: How he went on about's club money. Shall ter

come wi' me?

MINNIE: I wanted to do my curtains.

LUTHER: But tha's got a' day to do them in.

MINNIE: But I want to do them to-night—I feel like it.

LUTHER: A' right.—I shanna be long, at any rate.

> *A pause.*

What dost keep lookin' at?

MINNIE: How?

LUTHER: Tha keeps thy eye on me rarely.

MINNIE (*laughing*): It's your mouth—it looks *so* red and bright, in your black face.

LUTHER: Does it look nasty to thee?

MINNIE: No—no-o.

LUTHER (*pushing his moustache, laughing*): It ma'es you look like a nigger, i' your pit-dirt—th' whites o' your eyes!

MINNIE: Just.

> *She gets up to take his plate; goes and stands beside him. He lifts his face to her.*

I want to see if I can see you; you look so different.

LUTHER: Tha can see me well enough. Why dost want to?

MINNIE: It's almost like having a stranger.

LUTHER: Would ter rather?

MINNIE: What?

LUTHER: Ha'e a stranger?

MINNIE: What for?

LUTHER: Hao—I dunno.

MINNIE (*touching his hair*): You look rather nice—an' your hair's so dirty.

LUTHER: Gi'e me a kiss.

MINNIE: But where? You're all grime.

LUTHER: I'm sure I've licked my mouth clean.

MINNIE (*stooping suddenly, and kissing him*): You don't look nearly such a tame rabbit, in your pit-dirt.

LUTHER (*catching her in his arms*): Dunna I? (*Kisses her.*) What colour is my eyes?

MINNIE: Blue-grey.

LUTHER: An' thine's grey an' black.

MINNIE: Mind! (*She looks at her blouse when he releases her.*)

LUTHER (*timid*): Have I blacked it?

MINNIE: A bit.

   She goes to the scullery; returns with another dish.

LUTHER: They talkin' about comin' out again.

MINNIE (*returning*): Good laws!—they've no need.

LUTHER: They are, though.

MINNIE: It's a holiday they want.

LUTHER: Nay, it isna. They want th' proper scale here, just as they ha'e it ivrywhere else.

MINNIE: But if the seams are thin, and the company can't afford.

LUTHER: They can afford a' this gret new electric plant; they can afford to build new houses for managers, an' ter give blo— ter give Frazer twelve hundred a year.

MINNIE: If they want a good manager to make the pits pay, they have to give him a good salary.

LUTHER: So's he can clip down our wages.

MINNIE: Why, what are yours clipped down?

LUTHER: Mine isn't, but there's plenty as is.

MINNIE: And will this strike make a butty of you?

LUTHER: You don't strike to get made a butty on.

MINNIE: Then how *do* you do it? You're thirty-one.

LUTHER: An' there's many as owd as me as is day-men yet.

MINNIE: But there's more that aren't, that are butties.

LUTHER: Ay, they've had luck.

MINNIE: Luck! You mean they've had some *go* in them.

LUTHER: Why, what can I do more than I am doin'?

MINNIE: It isn't what you do, it's how you do it. Sluther through any job; get to th' end of it, no matter how. That's you.

LUTHER: I hole a stint as well as any man.

MINNIE: Then I back it takes you twice as long.

LUTHER: Nay, nor that either.

MINNIE: I *know* you're not much of a workman—I've heard it from other butties, that you never put your heart into anything.

LUTHER: Who has heard it fra?

MINNIE: From those that know. And I could ha' told it *them*, for I know you. You'll be a day-man at seven shillings a day till the end of your life—and you'll be satisfied, so long as you can shilly-shally through. That's what your mother did for you—mardin' you up till you were all mard-soft.

LUTHER: Tha's got a lot ter say a' of a suddin. Thee shut thy mouth.

MINNIE: You've been dragged round at your mother's apron-strings, all the lot of you, till there isn't half a man among you.

LUTHER: Tha seems fond enough of our Joe.

MINNIE: He is th' best in the bunch.

LUTHER: Tha should ha' married him, then.

MINNIE: I shouldn't have had to ask *him*, if he was ready.

LUTHER: I'd axed thee twice afore—tha knowed tha could ha'e it when ter wanted.

MINNIE: *Axed* me! It was like asking me to pull out a tooth for you.

LUTHER: Yi, an' it felt like it.

MINNIE: What?

LUTHER: Axin' thee to marry me. I'm blessed if it didna feel like axin' the doctor to pull ten teeth out of a stroke.

MINNIE: And then you expect me to have you!

LUTHER: Well, tha *has* done, whether or not.

MINNIE: I—yes, I had to fetch you, like a mother fetches a kid from school. A pretty sight you looked. Didn't your mother give you a ha'penny to spend, to get you to go?

LUTHER: No; she spent it for me.

MINNIE: She would! She wouldn't even let you spend your own ha'penny. You'd have lost it, or let somebody take it from you.

LUTHER: Yi. Thee.

MINNIE: Me!—me take anything from you! Why, you've got nothing worth having.

LUTHER: I dunno—tha seems ter think so sometimes.

MINNIE: Oh! Shilly-shally and crawl, that's all you can do. You ought to have stopped with your mother.

LUTHER: I should ha' done, if tha hadna hawksed me out.

MINNIE: You aren't *fit* for a woman to have married, you're not.

LUTHER: Then why did thee marry me? It wor thy doin's.

MINNIE: Because I could get nobody better.

LUTHER: I'm more class than I thought for, then.

MINNIE: Are you! Are you!

JOE'S voice is heard.

JOE: I'm comin' in, you two, so stop snaggin' an' snarlin'.

LUTHER: Come in; 'er'll 'appen turn 'er tap on thee.

JOE enters.

JOE: Are you eatin' yet?

LUTHER: Ay—it ta'es 'er that long ter tell my sins. Tha's just come right for puddin'. Get thee a plate outer t'cupboard— an' a spoon outer t'basket.

JOE (*at the cupboard*): You've got ivrythink tip-top. What should ter do if I broke thee a plate, Minnie?

MINNIE: I should break another over your head.

He deliberately drops and smashes a plate. She flushes crimson.

LUTHER: Well, I'm glad it worna me.

JOE: I'm that clumsy wi' my left 'and, Minnie! Why doesna ter break another ower my head?

LUTHER (*rising and putting pudding on a plate*): Here, ta'e this an' sit thee down.

His brother seats himself.

Hold thy knees straight, an' for God's sake dunna thee break this. Can ter manage?

JOE: I reckon so. If I canna, Minnie'll feed me wi' a spoon. Shonna ter?

MINNIE: Why did you break my plate?

JOE: Nay, I didna break it—it wor the floor.

MINNIE: You did it on purpose.

JOE: How could I? I didn't say ter th' floor: 'Break thou this plate, O floor!'

MINNIE: You have no right.

JOE (*addressing the floor*): Tha'd no right to break that plate— dost hear? I'd a good mind ter drop a bit o' puddin' on thy face.

He balances the spoon; the plate slides down from his knee, smash into the fender.

MINNIE (*screams*): It's my best service! (*Begins to sob.*)

LUTHER: Nay, our Joe!

JOE: 'Er's no occasions ter scraight. I bought th' service an' I can get th' plates matched. What's her grizzlin' about?

MINNIE: I shan't ask you to get them matched.

JOE: Dunna thee, an' then tha runs no risk o' bein' denied.

MINNIE: What have you come here like this for?

JOE: I haena come here like this. I come ter tell yer our Harriet says, would yer mind goin' an' tellin' 'er what she can do with that childt's coat, as she's made a' wrong. If you'd looked slippy, I'd ha' ta'en yer ter th' Cinematograph after. But, dearly-beloved brethren, let us weep; these our dear departed dinner-plates . . . Come, Minnie, drop a tear as you pass by.

LUTHER (*to* MINNIE): Tha needna fret, Minnie, they can easy be matched again.

MINNIE: You're just pleased to see him make a fool of me, aren't you?

LUTHER: He's non made a fool o' thee—tha's made a fool o' thysen, scraightin' an' carryin' on.

JOE: It's a fact, Minnie. Nay, let me kiss thee better.

She has risen, with shut face.

He approaches with outstretched left arm. She swings round, fetches him a blow over his upper right arm. He bites his lip with pain.

LUTHER (*rising*): Has it hurt thee, lad? Tha shouldna fool wi' her.

MINNIE *watches the two brothers with tears of mortification in her eyes. Then she throws off her apron, pins on her hat, puts on her coat, and is marching out of the house.*

LUTHER: Are you going to Harriet's?

JOE: I'll come and fetch you in time for th' Cinematograph.
The door is heard to bang.

JOE (*picking up broken fragments of plates*): That's done it.

LUTHER: It's bad luck—ne'er mind. How art goin' on?

JOE: Oh, all right.

LUTHER: What about thy club money?

JOE: They wunna gi'e't me. But, I say, sorry—tha'rt for it.

LUTHER: Ay—I dunno what 'er married me for, f'r it's nowt bu' fault she finds wi' me, from th' minnit I come i' th' house to th' minnit I leave it.

JOE: Dost wish tha'd niver done it?—niver got married?

LUTHER (*sulky*): I dunno—sometimes.

JOE (*with tragic emphasis*): Then it's the blasted devil!

LUTHER: I dunno—I'm married to 'er, an' she's married to me, so she can pick holes i' me as much as she likes——

JOE: As a rule, she's nice enough wi' me.

LUTHER: She's nice wi' ivrybody but me.

JOE: An' dost ter care?

LUTHER: Ay—I do.

JOE: Why doesn't ter go out an' leave her?

LUTHER: I dunno.

JOE: By the Lord, she'd cop it if I had 'er.
Pause.

LUTHER: I wor comin' up to-night.

JOE: I thought tha would be. But there's Mrs Purdy comin' ter see thee.

LUTHER: There's who?

JOE: Mrs Purdy. Didna ter ha'e a bit of a go wi' their Bertha, just afore Minnie wrote thee?

LUTHER: Ay. Why?

JOE: 'Er mother says she's wi' childt by thee. She come up ter my mother this afternoon, an' said she wor comin' here to-night.

LUTHER: Says what?

JOE: Says as their Bertha's goin' ter ha'e a child, an' 'er lays it on ter thee.

LUTHER: Oh, my good God!

JOE: Isna it right?

LUTHER: It's right if 'er says so.

JOE: Then it's the blasted devil! (*A pause.*) So I come on here ter see if I could get Minnie to go up to our Harriet.

LUTHER: Oh, my good God!

JOE: I thought, if we could keep it from 'er, we might settle summat, an' 'er niver know.

LUTHER (*slowly*): My God alive!

JOE: She said she'd hush it up, an' lay it ont'r a electrician as laid th' cable, an' is gone goodness knows where—make an arrangement, for forty pound.

LUTHER (*thoughtfully*): I wish I wor struck dead.

JOE: Well, tha arena', an' so tha'd better think about it. My mother said as Minnie ought to know, but I say diff'rent, an' if Mrs Purdy doesna tell her, nobody need.

LUTHER: I wish I wor struck dead. I wish a ton o' rock 'ud fa' on me to-morrer.

JOE: It wunna for wishin'.

LUTHER: My good God!

JOE: An' so—I'll get thee forty quid, an' lend it thee. When Mrs Purdy comes, tell her she shall ha'e twenty quid this day week, an' twenty quid a year from now, if thy name's niver been mentioned. I believe 'er's a clat-fart.

LUTHER: Me a childt by Bertha Purdy! But—but what's

that for—now there's Minnie?

JOE: I dunno what it's for, but theer it is, as I'm tellin' thee. I'll stop for another haef an hour, an' if 'er doesna come, than mun see to 'er by thysen.

LUTHER: 'Er'll be back afore ha'ef an hour's up. Tha mun go an' stop 'er . . . I—I niver meant—— Look here, our Joe, I—if I—if she—if she—— My God, what have I done now!

JOE: We can stop her from knowin'.

LUTHER (looking round): She'll be comin' back any minnit. Nay, I niver meant t'r ha'. Joe . . .

JOE: What?

LUTHER: She—she——

JOE: 'Er niver ned know.

LUTHER: Ah, but though . . .

JOE: What?

LUTHER: I—I—I've done it.

JOE: Well, it might ha' happened t'r anybody.

LUTHER: But when 'er knows—an' it's me as has done it . . .

JOE: It wouldn't ha' mattered o' anyhow, if it had bin sumb'dy else. But tha knows what ter's got ter say. Arena' ter goin' ter wesh thee? Go an' get th' panchion.

LUTHER (rising): 'Er'll be comin' in any minnit.

JOE: Get thee weshed, man.

LUTHER (fetching a bucket and lading-can from the scullery, and emptying water from the boiler): Go an' ta'e 'er somewhere, while Mrs Purdy goes, sholl ter?

JOE: D'rectly. Tha heered what I telled thee?

There is a noise of splashing in the scullery. Then a knock.
JOE goes to the door. He is heard saying 'Come in'.
Enter MRS PURDY.

MRS PURDY: I hope I've not come a-mealtimes.

JOE: No, they've finished. Minnie's gone up t'r our Harriet's.

MRS PURDY: Thank the Lord for small mercies—for I didn't fancy sittin' an' tellin' her about our Bertha.

JOE: We dunna want 'er ter know. Sit thee down.

MRS PURDY: I'm not of that mind, mester, I am. As I said, what's th' good o' jackin' up a young married couple? For it won't unmarry 'em nor ma'e things right. An' yet, my long lass oughtner ter bear a' th' brunt.

JOE: Well, an' 'er isna goin' to.

MRS PURDY: Is that Mester weshin'?

JOE: Ah.

MRS PURDY: 'As ter towd him?

JOE: Ah.

MRS PURDY: Well, it's none o' my wishin's, I'm sure o' that. Eh, dear, you've bin breakin' th' crockery a'ready!

JOE: Yes, that's me, bein' wallit.

MRS PURDY: T-t-t! So this is 'ow she fancied it?

JOE: Ah, an' it non luiks bad, does it?

MRS PURDY: Very natty. Very nice an' natty.

JOE (*taking up the lamp*): Come an' look at th' parlour.

JOE *and* MRS PURDY *exit R.*

MRS PURDY'S VOICE: Yis—yis—it's nice an' plain. But a bit o' red plush is 'andsomer, to my mind. It's th'old-fashioned style, like! My word, but them three ornyments is gaudy-lookin'.

JOE: An' they reckon they're worth five pound. 'Er mester gen 'em 'er.

MRS PURDY: I'd rather had th' money.

JOE: Ah, me an' a'.

During this time, LUTHER *has come hurrying out of the scullery into the kitchen, rubbing his face with a big roller-towel. He is naked to the waist. He kneels with his knees on the fender, sitting on his heels, rubbing himself. His back is not washed. He rubs his hair dry.*

Enter JOE, *with the lamp, followed by* MRS PURDY.

MRS PURDY: It's uncommon, very uncommon, Mester Gaskin—and looks well, too, for them as likes it. But it hardly goes wi' my fancy, somehow, startin' wi' second-hand, owd-fashioned stuff. You dunno *who's* sotten themselves on these 'ere chairs, now, do you?

LUTHER: It ma'es no diff'rence to me who's sot on 'em an' who 'asna.

MRS PURDY: No—you get used to'm.

LUTHER (*to* JOE): Shall thee go up t'r our Harriet's?

JOE: If ter's a mind. (*Takes up his cap. To* MRS PURDY): An' you two can settle as best you can.

MRS PURDY: Yes—yes. I'm not one for baulkin' mysen an' cuttin' off my nose ter spite my face.

   LUTHER *has finished wiping himself. He takes a shifting shirt from the bureau, and struggles into it; then goes into the scullery.*

JOE: An' you sure you'll keep it quiet, missis?

MRS PURDY: Am I goin' bletherin' up street an' down street, think yer?

JOE: An' dunna tell your Bob.

MRS PURDY: I've more sense. There's not a word 'e 'ears a-whoam as is of any count, for out it 'ud leak when he wor canned. Yes, my guyney—we know what our mester is.

   Re-enter LUTHER, *in shirt and black trousers. He drops his pit-trousers and singlet beside the hearth.*

   MRS PURDY *bends down and opens his pit-trousers.*

MRS PURDY: Nay, if ter drops 'em of a heap, they niver goin' ter get dry an' cosy. Tha sweats o' th' hips, as my lads did.

LUTHER: Well, go thy ways, Joe.

JOE: Ay—well—good luck. An' good night, Mrs Purdy.

MRS PURDY: Good night.

   Exit JOE.

   There are several moments of silence.

   LUTHER *puts the broken pots on the table.*

MRS PURDY: It's sad work, Mester Gaskin, f'r a' on us.

LUTHER: Ay.

MRS PURDY: I left that long lass o' mine fair gaunt, fair

chalked of a line, I did, poor thing. Not bu' what 'er should
'a 'ad more sense.

LUTHER: Ah!

MRS PURDY: But it's no use throwin' good words after bad
deeds. Not but what it's a nasty thing for yer t'r 'a done,
it is—an' yer can scarce look your missis i' th' face again, I
should think. (*Pause.*) But I says t'r our Bertha, 'It's his'n,
an' he mun pay!' Eh, but how 'er did but scraight an' cry.
It fair turned me ower. 'Dunna go to 'm, Mother,' 'er says,
'dunna go to 'm for to tell him!' 'Yi,' I says, 'right's right—
tha doesna get off wi' nowt, nor shall 'e neither. 'E wor
but a scamp to do such a thing,' I says, yes, I did. For you
was older nor 'er. Not but what she was old enough ter
ha'e more sense. But 'er wor allers one o' th' come-day
go-day sort, as 'ud gi'e th' clothes off 'er back an' niver
know 'er wor nek'd—a gra't soft looney as she is, an'
serves 'er right for bein' such a gaby. Yi, an' I believe 'er
wor fond on thee—if a wench can be fond of a married
man. For one blessing, 'er doesna know what 'er wor an'
what 'er worn't. For they mau talk o' bein' i' love—but
you non in love wi' onybody, wi'out they's a chance o'
their marryin' you—howiver much you may like 'em. An'
I'm thinkin', th' childt'll set 'er up again when it comes, for
'er's gone that wezzel-brained an' doited, I'm sure! An'
it's a mort o' trouble for me, mester, a sight o' trouble it is.
Nor as I s'll be hard on 'er. She knowed I wor comin' 'ere
to-night, an's not spoke a word for hours. I left 'er sittin'
on th' sofey hangin' 'er 'ead. But it's a weary business,
mester, an' nowt ter be proud on. I s'd think tha wishes
tha'd niver clapt eyes on our Bertha.

LUTHER (*thinking hard*): I dunna—I dunna. An' I dunna wish
as I'd niver seen 'er, no, I dunna. 'Er liked me, an' I liked 'er.

MRS PURDY: An' 'appen, but for this 'ere marriage o' thine,
tha'd 'a married 'er.

LUTHER: Ah, I should. F'r 'er liked me, an' 'er worna neither nice nor near, nor owt else, an' 'er'd bin fond o' me.

MRS PURDY: 'Er would, an' it's a thousand pities. But what's done's done

LUTHER: Ah, I know that.

MRS PURDY: An' as for yer missis——

LUTHER: 'Er mun do as 'er likes.

MRS PURDY: But tha'rt not for tellin' 'er?

LUTHER: 'Er—'er'll know some time or other.

MRS PURDY: Nay, nay, 'er nedna. You married now, lad, an' you canna please yoursen.

LUTHER: It's a fact.

MRS PURDY: An' Lizzy Stapleton, she had forty pound wi' 'er lad, an' it's not as if you hadn't got money. An' to be sure, we've none.

LUTHER: No, an' I've none.

MRS PURDY: Yes, you've some atween you—an'—well . . .

LUTHER: I can get some.

MRS PURDY: Then what do you say?

LUTHER: I say as Bertha's welcome t'r any forty pounds, if I'd got it. For—for—missis, she wor better to me than iver my wife's bin.

MRS PURDY (*frightened by his rage*): Niver, lad!

LUTHER: She wor—ah but though she wor. She thought a lot on me.

MRS PURDY: An' so I'm sure your missis does. She naggles thy heart out, maybe. But that's just the wrigglin' a place out for hersen. She'll settle down comfortable, lad.

LUTHER (*bitterly*): Will she!

MRS PURDY: Yi—yi. An' tha's done 'er a crewel wrong, my lad. An' tha's done my gel one as well. For, though she was old enough to know better, yet she's good-hearted and trusting, an' 'ud gi'e 'er shoes off 'er feet. An' tha's landed 'er, tha knows. For it's not th' bad women as 'as bastards nowadays—they've a sight too much gumption. It's fools like our'n—poor thing.

LUTHER: I've done everything that was bad, I know that.

MRS PURDY: Nay—nay—young fellers, they are like that. But it's wrong, for look at my long lass sittin' theer on that sofey, as if 'er back wor broke.

LUTHER (*loudly*): But I dunna wish I'd niver seen 'er, I dunna. It wor—it wor—she wor good to me, she wor, an' I dunna wish I'd niver done it.

MRS PURDY: Then tha ought, that's a'. For I do—an' 'er does.

LUTHER: Does 'er say 'er wishes 'er'd niver seen me?

MRS PURDY: 'Er says nowt o' nohow.

LUTHER: Then 'er doesna wish it. An' I wish I'd ha' married 'er.

MRS PURDY: Come, my lad, come. Married tha art——

LUTHER (*bitterly*): Married I am, an' I wish I worna. Your Bertha 'er'd 'a thought a thousand times more on me than *she* does. But I'm wrong, wrong, wrong, i' ivry breath I take. An' I will be wrong, yi, an' I *will* be wrong.

MRS PURDY: Hush thee—there's somebody comin'.

They wait.

Enter JOE *and* MINNIE, JOE *talking loudly.*

MINNIE: No, you've not, you've no right at all. (*To* LUTHER): Haven't you even cleared away? (*To* MRS PURDY): Good evening.

MRS PURDY: Good evenin', missis. I was just goin'—I've bin sayin' it looks very nice, th' 'ouse.

MINNIE: Do you think so?

MRS PURDY: I do, indeed.

MINNIE: Don't notice of the mess we're in, shall you? *He* (*pointing to* JOE) broke the plates—and then I had to rush off up to Mrs Preston's afore I could clear away. And he hasn't even mended the fire.

LUTHER: I can do—I niver noticed.

MINNIE (*to* MRS PURDY): Have a piece of cake? (*Goes to cupboard.*)

MRS PURDY: No, thanks, no, thanks. I mun get off afore th'

Co-op shuts up. Thank yer very much. Well, good night, all.

JOE *opens the door;* MRS PURDY *goes out.*

MINNIE (*bustling, clearing away as* LUTHER *comes in with coals*): Did you settle it?

LUTHER: What?

MINNIE: What she'd come about.

LUTHER: Ah.

MINNIE: An' I bet you'll go and forget.

LUTHER: Oh ah!

MINNIE: And poor old Bob Purdy will go on just the same.

LUTHER: Very likely.

MINNIE: Don't let the dust all go on the hearth. Why didn't you clear away? The house was like a pigsty for her to come into.

LUTHER: Then I wor the pig.

MINNIE (*halting*): Why—who's trod on your tail now?

LUTHER: There'd be nobody to tread on it if tha wor out.

MINNIE: Oh—oh, dearo' me. (*To* JOE): I think we'd better go to the Cinematograph, and leave him to nurse his sore tail.

JOE: We better had.

LUTHER: An' joy go with yer.

MINNIE: We certainly shan't leave it at home. (*To* JOE.) What time does it begin?

JOE: Seven o'clock.

MINNIE: And I want to call in Sisson's shop. Shall you go with me, or wouldn't you condescend to go shopping with me? (*She has cleared the table, brought a tray and a bowl, and is washing up the pots.*)

JOE: Dost think I'm daunted by Polly Sisson?

MINNIE: You're braver than most men if you dare go in a shop. Here, take a towel and wipe these pots.

JOE: How can I?

MINNIE: If you were a gentleman, you'd hold the plates in

your teeth to wipe them.

JOE: Tha wouldna look very ladylike at th' end on't.

MINNIE: Why?

JOE: Why, has forgot a'ready, what a shine tha kicked up when I broke them two other plates? (*He has got a towel, and wedging a plate against his thighs, is laboriously wiping it.*)

MINNIE: I never kicked up a shine. It *is* nice of you!

JOE: What?

MINNIE: To do this for me.

> LUTHER *has begun sweeping the hearth.*

JOE: Tha's got two servants.

MINNIE: But I'm sure you want to smoke while you're doing it—don't you now?

JOE: Sin' tha says so. (*Fumbles in his pocket.*)

MINNIE (*hastily wiping her hands, puts a cigarette between his lips—gets matches from the mantelpiece, ignoring her husband, who is kneeling sweeping the hearth—lights his cigarette*): It's so nice to have a lamed man. You feel you've got an excuse for making a fuss of him. You've got awfully nice eyes and eyebrows. I like dark eyes.

JOE: Oh ah!

> LUTHER *rises hastily, goes in the passage, crosses the room quietly. He wears his coat, a red scarf and a cap.*

MINNIE: There's more go in them than in blue. (*Watches her husband go out. There is silence between the two.*)

JOE: He'll come round again.

MINNIE: He'll have to. He'll go on sulking now. (*Her face breaks.*) You—you don't know how hard it is.

JOE: What?

MINNIE (*crying a few fierce tears*): This . . .

JOE (*aghast*): What?

MINNIE: Why—don't you know. You don't know how hard it is, with a man as—as leaves you alone all the time.

JOE: But—he niver hardly goes out.

MINNIE: No, but—you don't know—he leaves me alone, he

always has done—and there's nobody . . .

JOE: But he . . .

MINNIE: He never trusts me—he leaves me so alone—and—
(*a little burst of tears*) it *is* hard! (*She changes suddenly.*) You've
wiped your plates; my word, you are a champion.

JOE: I think so an' a'.

MINNIE: I hope the pictures will be jolly—but the sad ones
make me laugh more, don't they you?

JOE: I canna do wi' 'em.

CURTAIN

ACT TWO

The same evening—eleven o'clock. LUTHER'S *house.*

MINNIE, *alone, weeping. She gets up, fills the kettle, puts it on the hob, sits down, weeps again; then hears somebody coming, dries her eyes swiftly, turns the lamp low.*

Enter LUTHER. *He stands in the doorway—is rather tipsy; flings his cap down, sits in his chair, lurching it slightly. Neither speaks for some moments.*

LUTHER: Well, did yer like yer pictures?

MINNIE: Where have you been?

LUTHER: What does it matter where I've been?

MINNIE: Have you been drinking?

LUTHER: What's it matter if I have?

MINNIE: It matters a lot to me.

LUTHER: Oh ah!

MINNIE: Do you think I'm going to sleep with a man who is half-drunk?

LUTHER: Nay, I non know who tha'rt goin' ter sleep wi'.

MINNIE (*rising*): I shall make the bed in the other room.

LUTHER: Tha's no 'casions. I s'll do very nicely on t' sofa; it's warmer.

MINNIE: Oh, you can have your own bed.

LUTHER: If tha doesna sleep in it, I dunna.

MINNIE: And if *you do*, I don't.

LUTHER: Tha pleases thysen. Tha can sleep by thysen for iver, if ter's a mind to't.

MINNIE (*who has stood hesitating*): Oh, very well!

She goes upstairs, returns immediately with a pillow and two blankets, which she throws on the sofa.

LUTHER: Thank yer kindly.

MINNIE: Shall you rake?

LUTHER: I'll rake.

She moves about; lays table for his morning's breakfast: a newspaper, cup, plate, etc.—no food, because it would go dry; rinses his tin pit-bottle, puts it and his snap-bag on the table.

I could do it for mysen. Tha ned do nowt for me.

MINNIE: Why this sudden fit of unselfishness?

LUTHER: I niver want thee to do nowt for me, niver no more. No, not so much as lift a finger for me—not if I wor dyin'.

MINNIE: You're not dying; you're only tipsy.

LUTHER: Well, it's no matter to thee what I am.

MINNIE: It's very comfortable for you to think so.

LUTHER: I know nowt about that.

MINNIE (*after a pause*): Where have you been to-night?

LUTHER: There an' back, to see how far it is.

MINNIE (*making an effort*): Have you been up to your mother's?

LUTHER: Where I've bin, I've bin, and where I haven't, I haven't.

MINNIE: Pah!—you needn't try to magnify it and make a mountain. You've been to your mother's, and then to 'The Ram'.

LUTHER: All right—if tha knows, tha knows, an' theer's an end on't.

MINNIE: You talk like a fool.

LUTHER: That comes o' bein' a fool.

MINNIE: When were you a fool?

LUTHER: Ivry day o' my life, an' ivry breath I've ta'en.

MINNIE (*having finished work, sits down again*): I suppose you haven't got it in you to say anything fresh.

LUTHER: Why, what dost want me ter say? (*He looks at her for the first time.*)

MINNIE (*with a queer catch*): You might be more of a man if you said you were sorry.

LUTHER: Sorry! Sorry for what?

MINNIE: You've nothing to be sorry *for*, have you?

LUTHER (*looking at her, quickly*): What art goin' ter say?

MINNIE: It's what are *you* going to say. (*A silence.*)

LUTHER (*doggedly*): I'm goin' ter say nowt.

MINNIE (*bitterly*): No, you're not *man* enough to say anything
—you can only slobber. You do a woman a wrong, but
you're never man enough to say you're sorry for it. You're
not a man, you're not—you're something crawling!

LUTHER: I'm glad! I'm glad! I'm glad! No, an' I wouldna
ta'e't back, no. 'Er wor nice wi' me, which is a thing tha's
niver bin. An' so tha's got it, an' mun keep it.

MINNIE: Who was nice with you?

LUTHER: *She* was—an' would ha'e bin at this minnit, but for
thee.

MINNIE: Pah!—you're not fit to have a wife. You only want
your mother to rock you to sleep.

LUTHER: Neither mother, nor wife, neither thee nor onybody
do I want—no—no.

MINNIE: No—you've had three cans of beer.

LUTHER: An' if ter niver sleeps i' th' bed wi' me again, an' if
ter niver does a hand's turn for me niver no more, I'm glad,
I'm glad. I non want thee. I non want ter see thee.

MINNIE: You mean coward. Good God! I never thought you
were such a mean coward as this.

LUTHER: An' as for thy money—yi, I wouldna smell on't.
An' neither thine, nor our Joe's, nor my mother's will I ha'e.
What I addle's my own. What I gi'e thee, I gie thee. An'
she maun ha'e ten shillin's a month, an' tha maun abide by't.

MINNIE: What are you talking about?

LUTHER: My mother wouldna gi'e me th' money. She says
she's done her share. An' tha's done thine. An' I've done
mine, begod. An' what yer canna chew yer maun swaller.

MINNIE: You must be quite drunk.

LUTHER: Must I? All right, it's Dutch courage then. A'right,
then Dutch courage it is. But I tell thee, tha does as ter's a

mind. Tha can leave me, an' go back inter service, if ter wants. What's it ter me, if I'm but a lump o' suck i' th' 'ouse wheer tha art? Tha should ha' had our Joe—he's got more go than me. An' I should ha' had 'er. I'd got go enough for *her*; 'appen a bit too much.

MINNIE: Her? Who?

LUTHER: Her! An' I'm glad 'er's wi' my childt. I'm glad I did it. I'm glad! For tha's wiped tha feet on me enough. Yi, tha's wiped thy feet on me till what's it to me if tha does it or not? It isna! An' now—tha maun abide by what ter's got, tha maun. I s'll ha'e to—an' by plenty I handna got I've abided. An' so—an' so—yi.

MINNIE: But who is it you—who is she?

LUTHER: Tha knowed a' along.

MINNIE: Who is it?

They are both silent.

Aren't you going to speak?

LUTHER: What's the good?

MINNIE (*coldly*): But I must know.

LUTHER: Tha does know.

MINNIE: I can assure you I don't.

LUTHER: Then assure thysen an' find out.

Another silence.

MINNIE: Do you mean somebody is going to have a baby by you?

LUTHER: I mean what I've said, an' I mean nowt else.

MINNIE: But you must tell me.

LUTHER: I've boiled my cabbage twice a'ready, hanna I?

MINNIE: Do you mean somebody is going to have a child by you?

LUTHER: Tha can chew it ower, if ter's a mind.

MINNIE (*helpless*): But . . . (*She struggles with herself, then goes calm.*)

LUTHER: That's what I say—*but* . . . !

A silence.

MINNIE: And who is she?

LUTHER: Thee, for a' I know.

MINNIE (*calmly, patiently*): I asked you a question.

LUTHER: Ah—an' I 'eered thee.

MINNIE: Then answer me—who is she?

LUTHER: Tha knows well enow—tha knowed afore they'd towd thee——

MINNIE: Nobody has told me. Who is she?

LUTHER: Well, tha's seed 'er mother.

MINNIE (*numb*): Mrs Purdy?

LUTHER: Yi.

MINNIE: Their Bertha?

LUTHER: Yi.

   A silence.

MINNIE: Why didn't you tell me?

LUTHER: Tell thee what?

MINNIE: This.

LUTHER: Tha knowed afore I did.

MINNIE: I know *now*.

LUTHER: Me an' a'.

   A pause.

MINNIE: Didn't you know till to-night?

LUTHER: Our Joe told me when tha'd just gone—I niver dreamt afore—an' then 'er mother . . .

MINNIE: What did her mother come for?

LUTHER: Ter see if we could hush it up a'cause o' thee, an' gi'e 'er a lump sum.

MINNIE: Hush it up because of me?

LUTHER: Ah—lay it ont'r an electrician as wor wi' th' gang as laid th' cable down to Balford—he's gone God knows where.

MINNIE: But it's yours.

LUTHER: I know that.

MINNIE: Then why lay it onto somebody else?

LUTHER: Because o' thee.

MINNIE: But why because of me?

LUTHER: To stop thee knowin', I s'd think.

MINNIE: And why shouldn't I know?

LUTHER: Eh, I dunno.

A pause.

MINNIE: And what were you going to do to stop me knowing?

LUTHER: 'Er axed for forty pounds down.

MINNIE: And if you paid forty pounds, you got off scot-free?

LUTHER: Summat so.

MINNIE: And where were the forty pounds coming from?

LUTHER: Our Joe said 'e'd lend 'em me. I thought my mother would, but 'er said 'er wouldna—neither would she gi'e't our Joe ter lend me, she said. For I wor a married man now, an' it behoved my wife to look after me. An' I thought tha knowed. I thought th'ad twigged, else bin telled. An' I didna care, an' dunna care.

MINNIE: And this is what you married me to!

LUTHER: This is what tha married me to. But I'll niver ax thee for, no, not so much as the liftin' of a finger—no——

MINNIE: But when you wrote and told me you were willing to marry me, why didn't you tell me this?

LUTHER: Because—as I've telled thee—I didna know till this very mortal night.

MINNIE: But you knew you'd been with her.

LUTHER: Ay, I knowed that.

A pause.

MINNIE: And why didn't you tell me?

LUTHER: What for should I tell thee? What good would it ha' done thee? Tha niver towd *me* nowt.

MINNIE: So that is how you look at it?

LUTHER: I non care how I look at it.

A pause.

MINNIE And was there anybody else?

LUTHER: How dost mean?

MINNIE: Have you been with any other woman?

LUTHER: I dunno—I might—I dunno.

MINNIE: That means you have.

LUTHER: I'm thirty.

MINNIE: And who *were* they?

LUTHER: I dunno. I've niver bin much wi' anybody—little, very little—an' then it wor an off-chance. Our Joe wor more that way than me—I worn't that way.

> *A pause.*

MINNIE: So—this was what I waited for you for!

LUTHER: Yha niver waited for me. Tha had me a'cause tha couldna get nobody better.

MINNIE: And so——

LUTHER (*after a moment*): Yi, an' so. An' so, I non care what ter does. If ter leaves me——

MINNIE (*in a flash*): What's the good of me leaving you? Aren't I married to you—tied to you?

LUTHER: Tha could leave me whether or not. I should go t'r Australia wi' our Joe.

MINNIE: And what about that girl?

LUTHER: I should send 'er th' money.

MINNIE: And what about me?

LUTHER: Tha'd please thysen.

MINNIE: Should you *like* me to leave you, and let you go to Australia?

LUTHER: 'Appen I should.

MINNIE: What did you marry me for?

LUTHER: 'Cos tha axed me.

MINNIE: Did you ever care for me?

> *He does not answer.*

Didn't you?

> *He does not answer.*

Didn't you?

LUTHER (*slowly*): You niver wanted me—you thought me dirt.

MINNIE: Ha! (*A pause.*) You can have the forty pounds.

LUTHER (*very doggedly*): I shanna.

MINNIE: She's got to be paid.

LUTHER: Tha keeps thy money.

MINNIE: Then where shall you get it from?

LUTHER: I s'll pay 'er month by month.

MINNIE: But you can't. Think!

LUTHER: Then I'll borrow forty quid somewhere else, an' pay it back i' instalments. Tha keeps thy money.

MINNIE You can borrow it from me.

LUTHER: I shall not.

MINNIE: Very well. I only wanted not to have the bother of paying month by month. I think I shall go back to my old place.

LUTHER: Tha pleases thysen.

MINNIE: And you can go and live with your mother again.

LUTHER: That I should niver do—but tha pleases thysen. We've bin married seven wik come Tuesday.

MINNIE I niver ought to ha' done it.

LUTHER: What?

MINNIE: Married you.

LUTHER: No.

MINNIE: For you never cared enough.

LUTHER: Yi—it's my fault.

MINNIE: Yes.

LUTHER: It would be. Tha's niver made a fault i' thy life.

MINNIE: Who are you, to talk about my faults!

LUTHER: Well——

 A pause.

MINNIE: I shall write to Mr Westlake to-morrow.

LUTHER: Tha does as pleases thee.

MINNIE: And if they can't take me back straight away, I shall ask him if he knows another place.

LUTHER: A'right. An' we'll sell th' furniture.

MINNIE (*looking round at her home*): Yes.

LUTHER: It'll non bring ha'ef tha giv for't—but it'll bring enough ter ta'e me out theer.

MINNIE: I'll make up what you lose by it, since I chose it.

LUTHER: Tha can give ter them as'll ha'e.

MINNIE: But I shall feel I owe it you.

LUTHER: I've had six weeks o' married life wi' thee. I mun pay for that.

MINNIE: You are mean, mean.

LUTHER: I know—though tha'rt first as has told me so. When dost reckon tha'lt go?

MINNIE: I'll go to-morrow if you want to get rid of me.

LUTHER: Nay—tha does just as pleases thysen. I non want ter get rid on thee. Nay, nay, it's not that. It's thee as wants ter go.

MINNIE: At any rate, I s'll have a place inside a fortnight.

LUTHER (*dully*): All right.

MINNIE: So I shall have to trouble you till then.

LUTHER: But I dunna want thee ter do owt for me—no, I dunna.

MINNIE: I shall keep the house, in payment for my board and lodgings. And I'll make the bed up in the back room, and I'll sleep there, because it's not furnished, and the house is yours.

LUTHER: Th'art—tha'rt—I wish I might strike thee down!

MINNIE: And I shall keep the account of every penny I spend and you must just pay the bills.

LUTHER (*rising suddenly*): I'll murder thee afore tha does.

He goes out. She sits twisting her apron. He returns with a large lump of coal in his hands, and rakes the fire.

MINNIE: You cared more for her than for me.

LUTHER: For who?

MINNIE: For her. She was the sort of sawney you ought to have had. Did she think you perfect?

LUTHER (*with grim satisfaction*): She liked me.

MINNIE: And you could do just as you wanted with her?

LUTHER: She'd ha' done owt for me.

MINNIE: And it flattered you, did it? Because a long stalk wi' no flower was at your service, it flattered you, did it? My word, it ought—— As for your Joe, he's not a fool like you, and that's why women think more of him. He wouldn't want a Bertha Purdy. He'd get a woman who was something—and because he knew how to appreciate her. You—what good are you?

LUTHER: I'm no good, but to fetch an' carry.

MINNIE: And a tuppenny scullery-girl could do that as well.

LUTHER: All right.

MINNIE: I'll bet even Bertha Purdy thinks what a clown you are. She never wanted you to marry her, did she?

LUTHER: She knowed I wouldn't.

MINNIE: You flatter yourself. I'll bet she never wanted you. I shouldn't be surprised if the child isn't somebody else's, that she just foists on you because you're so soft.

LUTHER: Oh ah!

MINNIE: It even flatters you to think it's yours.

LUTHER: Oh ah!

MINNIE: And quite right too—for it's the only thing you could have to be proud of. And then really it's not you . . .

LUTHER: Oh ah!

MINNIE: If a woman has a child, and you think you're the cause, do you think it's *your* doings?

LUTHER: If tha has one, it will be.

MINNIE: And is *that* anything for you to be proud of? Me whom you've insulted and deceived and treated as no snail would treat a woman! And then you expect me to bear your children!

LUTHER: I dunna expect thee. If tha does tha does.

MINNIE: And you gloat over it and feel proud of it!

LUTHER: Yi, I do.

MINNIE: No—no! I'd rather have married a tramp off the

streets than you. And—and I don't believe you *can* have children.

LUTHER: Theer tha knows tha'rt a liar.

MINNIE: I hate you.

LUTHER: All right.

MINNIE: And I *will* leave you, I *will*.

LUTHER: Tha's said so afore.

MINNIE: And I mean it.

LUTHER: All right.

MINNIE: But it's your mother's doing. *She* mollycoddled and marded you till you weren't a man—and now—I have to pay for it.

LUTHER: Oh ah!

MINNIE: No, you're not a man!

LUTHER: All right. They's plenty of women as would say I am.

MINNIE: They'd be lying to get something out of you.

LUTHER: Why, what could they get outer me?

MINNIE: Yes—yes—what could they . . . (*She stutters to a close.*)

   He begins to take off his boots.

LUTHER: If tha'rt goin', tha'd better go afore th' strike begins. We should be on short commons then—ten bob a wik.

MINNIE: There's one thing, you'd be on short commons without me. For nobody would keep you for ten shillings a week, unless you went to your mother's.

LUTHER: I could live at our Harriet's, an' pay 'er off after. An' there'd be th' furniture sold.

MINNIE: And you'd be delighted if there *was* a strike, so you could loaf about. You don't even get drunk. You only loaf. You're lazy, lazy, and without the stomach of a louse. You *want* a strike.

LUTHER: All right.

MINNIE: And I hope you'll get what you deserve, I do.

LUTHER: Tha'rt gi'en it me.

MINNIE (*lifting her hand suddenly*): How *dare* you say so—
how *dare* you! I'm too good for you.

LUTHER (*sullenly*): I know.

MINNIE: Yes.

She gets a candle, lights it, and goes to bed. He flings off his scarf and coat and waistcoat, throws the pillow on the hearth-rug, wraps himself in the blankets, blows the lamp out, and lies down.

CURTAIN

ACT THREE

A fortnight later—afternoon. The kitchen of LUTHER GAS-
COIGNE'S *house.*

MRS GASCOIGNE, *senior, alone. Enter* MINNIE GASCOIGNE,
dressed from travelling. She is followed by a CABMAN *carrying
a bag.*

MRS GASCOIGNE: What—is it you!

MINNIE: Yes. Didn't you get my wire?

MRS GASCOIGNE: Thy wire! Dost mean a tallygram? No,
we'n had nowt though th' house 'as bin shut up.

MINNIE (*to the* CABMAN): Thank you. How much?

CABMAN: Ha'ef-a-crown.

MRS GASCOIGNE: Ha'ef-a-crown for commin' from th'
Midland station! Why, tha non know what's talkin' about.

MINNIE (*paying him*): Thank you.

CABMAN: Thank yer. Good afternoon.

The CABMAN *goes out.*

MRS GASCOIGNE: My word, tha knows how ter ma'e th'
money fly.

MINNIE: I couldn't carry a bag.

MRS GASCOIGNE: Tha could ha' come i' th' 'bus ter Eastwood an' then a man 'ud 'a browt it on.

MINNIE: It is raining.

MRS GASCOIGNE: Tha'rt neither sugar nor salt.

MINNIE: I wonder you didn't get my telegram.

MRS GASCOIGNE: I tell thee, th' 'ouse wor shut up last night.

MINNIE: Oh!

MRS GASCOIGNE: I dunno wheer 'e slep'—wi' some o's pals
I should think.

MINNIE: Oh!

MRS GASCOIGNE: Thinks I to mysen, I'd better go an' ge
some dinner ready down theer. So I told our Joe ter come
'ere for's dinner as well, but they'm neither on 'em bin in
yet. That's allers t'road when it's strike. They stop mormin'
about, bletherin' and boomin' an' meals, bless yer, they
don't count. Tha's bin i' Manchester four days then?

MINNIE: Yes.

MRS GASCOIGNE: Ay.—Our Luther's niver bin up ter tell
me. If I hadna ha' met Mrs Pervin fra next door here, I
should niver ha' knowed a word. That wor yisterday. So
I sent our Joe down. But it seems 'e's neither bin a-whoam
yesterday nor th' day afore. He slep' i' th' 'ouse by hissen
for two nights. So Mrs Sharley said. He said tha'd gone ter
Manchester on business.

MINNIE: Yes.

MRS GASCOIGNE: But he niver come ter tell *me* nowt on't.

MINNIE: Didn't he?

MRS GASCOIGNE: It's trew what they say:

'My son's my son till he ta'es him a wife,

But my daughter's my daughter the whole of her life.'

MINNIE: Do you think so?

MRS GASCOIGNE: I'm sure. An' th' men's been out ten days
now, an' such carryin's-on

MINNIE: Oh! Why—what?

MRS GASCOIGNE: Meetin's ivry mornin'—crier for ever
down th' street wi's bell—an' agitators. They say as Fraser
dursn't venture out o' th' door. Watna' pit-top's bin afire,
and there's a rigiment o' soldiers drillin' i' th' statutes
ground—bits o' things they are, an' a', like a lot o' little
monkeys i' their red coats—Staffordshire men. But wiry,
so they say. Same as marched wi' Lord Roberts to Candy-
har. But not a man among 'em. If you watch out fra th'
gardin end, you'll see 'em i' th' colliers' train goin' up th'
line ter Watna'—wi' their red coats jammed i' th' winders.
They say as Fraser's got ten on 'em in's house ter guard

him—an' they's sentinels at pit top, standin' wi' their guns,
an' th' men crackin' their sides wi' laughing at 'em.

MINNIE: What for?

MRS GASCOIGNE: Nay, that I canna tell thee. They've got
the Black Watch up at Heanor—so they says—great big
Scotchmen i' kilts. They look well, ha'en them i' Heanor,
wi' a' them lasses.

MINNIE: And what is all the fuss about?

MRS GASCOIGNE: Riotin'. I thought tha'd bobbled off ter
Manchester ter be i' safety.

MINNIE: Oh, no—I never knew there was any danger.

MRS GASCOIGNE: No more there is, as far as that goes.
What's up atween you an' our Luther?

MINNIE: Oh, nothing particular.

MRS GASCOIGNE: I knowed summat wor amiss, when 'e
niver come up. It's a fortnight last Tuesday, sin' 'e's set
foot i' my house—an' I've niver clapt eyes on him. I axed
our Joe, but he's as stubborn as a jackass, an' you canna
get a word out on 'im, not for love nor money.

MINNIE: Oh!

MRS GASCOIGNE: Talk's o' goin' t'r Australay. But not if
I can help it. An' hints as if our Luther—you not thinkin'
of it, are you?

MINNIE: No, I'm not—not that I know of.

MRS GASCOIGNE: H'm! It's a rum go, when nobody seems
ter know where they are, nor what they're goin' ter do.
But there's more blort than bustle, i' this world. What took
thee to Manchester?

MINNIE: Oh, I just wanted to go, on business.

MRS GASCOIGNE: Summat about thy money, like?

MINNIE: Yes.

MRS GASCOIGNE: Our Luther wor axin' me for forty pound,
th' last time 'e wor up—but I didna see it. No—I fun' him
a' as 'e wanted for's marriage, and gen 'im ten pound i'
hand, an' I thought it 'ud suffice. An' as for forty pound—

it's ter much, that's what I think.

MINNIE: I don't.

MRS GASCOIGNE: Oh, well, if tha doesna, a' well an' good. 'Appen he's paid it, then?

MINNIE: Paid it! Why. wheer was he to get it from?

MRS GASCOIGNE: I thought you had it atween you.

MINNIE: We haven't.

MRS GASCOIGNE: Why, how dost mean?

MINNIE: I mean we've neither of us got as much as forty pounds.

MRS GASCOIGNE: Dost mean *tha* hasna?

MINNIE: No, I haven't.

MRS GASCOIGNE: What's a-gait now?

MINNIE: Nothing.

MRS GASCOIGNE: What hast bin up to?

MINNIE: I? Nothing. I went to Manchester to settle a little business, that's all.

MRS GASCOIGNE: Ane wheer did ter stop?

MINNIE: I stayed with my old master.

MRS GASCOIGNE: Wor there no missis, then?

MINNIE: No—his wife is dead. You know I was governess for his grandchildren, who were born in India.

MRS GASCOIGNE: H'm! So tha went to see *him*?

MINNIE: Yes—I've always told him everything.

MRS GASCOIGNE: So tha went clat-fartin' ter 'im about our Luther, did ter?

MINNIE: Well—he's the only soul in the world that I *can* go to.

MRS GASCOIGNE: H'm! It doesna become thee, methinks.

MINNIE: Well!

Footsteps are heard.

MRS GASCOIGNE: Here's them lads, I s'd think.

Enter LUTHER *and* JOE.

JOE (*to* MINNIE): Hello! has thee come?

MINNIE: Yes. I sent a wire, and thought someone might

come to meet me.

JOE: Nay, there wor no wire. We thought tha'd gone for good.

MINNIE: Who thought so?

JOE: Well—didna tha say so?

MINNIE: Say what?

JOE: As tha'd go, an' he could do what he liked?

MINNIE: I've said many things.

MRS GASCOIGNE: So that was how it stood! Tha'rt a fool, our Luther. If ter ta'es a woman at 'er word, well, tha deserves what ter gets.

LUTHER: What am I to do, might I ax?

MRS GASCOIGNE: Nay, that thy wits should tell thee. Wheer hast bin these two days?

LUTHER: I walked ower wi' Jim Horrocks ter their Annie's i' Mansfield.

MRS GASCOIGNE: I'm sure she'd got enough to do, without two men planting themselves on her. An' how did ter get back?

LUTHER: Walked.

MRS GASCOIGNE: Trapsein' thy shoe-leather off thee feet, walkin' twenty miles. Has had thy dinner?

JOE: We've both had free dinners at th' Methodist Chapel.

LUTHER: I met Tom Heseldine i' 'Th' Badger Box', Mother.

MRS GASCOIGNE: Oh ay! Wide-mouthed as iver, I reckon.

JOE: Just same. But what dost think, Mother? It's leaked out as Fraser's got a lot o' chaps to go to-morrer mornin', ter see after th' roads an' a' that.

MRS GASCOIGNE: Th' roads wants keepin' safe, dunna they?

JOE: Yi—but if th' mesters wunna ha'e th' union men, let 'em do it theirselves.

MRS GASCOIGNE: Tha talks like a fool.

LUTHER: What right ha' they ter get a lot of scrawdrags an' blacklegs in ter do our work? A' th' pit maun fa' in, if they wunna settle it fair wi' us.

JOE: Then workin's is ours, an' th' mesters'. If th' mesters wunna treat us fair, then they mun keep 'em right theirselves. Thy non goin' ter ha'e no third body in.

MINNIE: But even when it's settled, how are you going back, if the roof has come in, and the roads are gone?

JOE: Tha mun ax th' mesters that. If we canna go back ter th' rotten owd pits no more, we mun look elsewhere. An' th' mesters can sit atop o' their pits an' stroke 'em.

LUTHER (to MINNIE): If I got a woman in to do th' housework as tha wunna do for me, tha'd sit smilin', shouldn't ter?

MINNIE: She could do as she liked.

LUTHER: All right. Then, Mother, 'appen tha'lt boss this house. She run off ter Manchester, an' left me ter starve. So 'appen tha'lt come an' do for me.

MRS GASCOIGNE: Nay—if ter wants owt tha mun come ter *me*.

JOE: That's right. Dunna thee play blackleg i' this establishment.

MRS GASCOIGNE: I s'll mind my own business.

JOE (to MINNIE): Now, does *thee* think it right, Minnie, as th' mesters should get a lot o' crawlin' buggers in ter keep their pits i' order. when th' keepin' o' them pits i' order belongs by right to us?

MINNIE: It belongs to whosoever the masters pay to do it.

LUTHER: A' right. Then it belongs to me to ha'e any woman in ter do for me, as I've a mind. Tha's gone on strike, so I ha'e the right ter get anybody else.

MINNIE: When have I gone on strike? I have always done your housework.

LUTHER: Housework—yi! But we dunna on'y keep th' roof from comin' in. We *get* as well. An' even th' housework tha went on strike wi'. Tha skedaddled off ter Manchester, an' left me to't.

MINNIE: I went on business.

LUTHER: An' we've come out on strike 'on business'.

MINNIE: You've not; it's a game.

LUTHER: An' the mesters'll ta'e us back when they're ready, or when they're forced to. An' same wi' thee by me.

MINNIE: Oh!

JOE: We got it fr' Tom Rooke—'e wor goin' ter turn 'em down. At four tomorrer mornin', there's ower twenty men goin' down.

MRS GASCOIGNE: What a lot of fools men are! As if th' pits didn't need ter be kep' tidy, ready for you to go back to'm.

JOE: They'll be kep' tidy by us, then an' when we've a mind—an' by nobody else.

MRS GASCOIGNE: Tha talks very high an' mighty. That's because I ha'e th' feedin' on thee.

JOE: You put it like our Luther says, then. He stands for t'mesters, an' Minnie stands for t'men—cos 'er's gone on strike. Now becos she's went ter Manchester, had he got only right ter ha'e Lizzie Charley in for a couple o' nights an' days?

MRS GASCOIGNE: Tha talks like a fool!

JOE: I dunna.

MINNIE: He's welcome to Lizzie Charley.

JOE: All right.—She's a nice gel. We'll ax 'er to come in an' manage th' 'ouse—he can pay 'er.

MINNIE: What with?

JOE: Niver you mind. Should yer like it?

MINNIE: He can do just as he likes.

JOE: Then should I fetch her?—should I, Luther?

LUTHER: If ter's a mind.

JOE: Should I, then, Minnie?

MINNIE: If he wants her.

LUTHER: I want somebody ter look after me.

JOE: Right tha art. (*Puts his cap on.*) I'll say as Minnie canna look after th' house, will 'er come. That it?

LUTHER: Ah.

MRS GASCOIGNE: Dunna be a fool. Tha's had a can or two.

JOE: Well—'er'll be glad o' the job.

MRS GASCOIGNE: You'd better stop him, one of you.

LUTHER: I want somebody ter look after me—an' tha wunna.

MRS GASCOIGNE: Eh dear o' me! Dunna thee be a fool, our Joe.

Exit JOE.

What wor this job about goin' ter Manchester?

LUTHER: She said she wouldna live wi' me, an' so 'er went. I thought 'er'd gone for good.

MINNIE: You didn't—you *knew*.

LUTHER: I knowed what tha'd towd me—as tha'd live wi' me no longer. Tha's come back o' thy own accord.

MINNIE: I never said I shouldn't come back.

LUTHER: Tha said as tha wouldna live wi' me. An' tha *didna*, neither,—not for——

MRS GASCOIGNE: Well, Minnie, you've brought it on your own head. You put him off, an' you put him off, as if 'e was of no account, an' then all of a sudden you invited him to marry you——

MINNIE: Put him off! He didn't need much putting off. He never came any faster than a snail.

MRS GASCOIGNE: Twice, to my knowledge, he axed thee—an' what can a man do more?

MINNIE: Yes, what! A gramophone in breeches could do as much.

MRS GASCOIGNE: Oh, indeed! What ailed him was, he wor in collier's britches, i'stead o' a stool-arsed Jack's.

MINNIE: No—what ailed him was that *you* kept him like a kid hanging on to you.

MRS GASCOIGNE: An' tha bit thy own nose off, when ter said him nay. For had ter married him at twenty-three, there'd ha' been none of this trouble.

MINNIE: And why didn't I? Why didn't I? Because he came in his half-hearted 'I will if you lie' fashion, and I despised him, yes I did.

MRS GASCOIGNE: And who are *you* to be despising him, I should like to know?

MINNIE: I'm a woman, and that's enough. But I know now, it was your fault. You held him, and persuaded him that what he wanted was *you*. You kept him, like a child, you even gave him what money he wanted, like a child. He never roughed it—he never faced out anything. You did all that for him.

MRS GASCOIGNE: And what if I did! If you made as good a wife to him as I made a mother, you'd do.

MINNIE: Should I? You didn't care what women your sons went with, so long as they didn't love them. What do you care really about this affair of Bertha Purdy? You don't. All you cared about was to keep your sons for yourself. You kept the solid meal, and the orts and slarts any other woman could have. But I tell you, I'm *not* for having the orts and slarts, and your leavings from your sons. I'll have a man, or nothing, I will.

MRS GASCOIGNE: It's rare to be some folks, ter pick and choose.

MINNIE: I can't pick and choose, no. But what I won't have, I won't have, and that is all.

MRS GASCOIGNE (*to* LUTHER): Have I ever kept thee from doin' as tha wanted? Have I iver marded and coddled thee?

LUTHER: Tha hasna, beguy!

MINNIE: No, you haven't, perhaps, not by the look of things. But you've bossed him. You've decided everything for him, really. He's depended on you as much when he was thirty as when he was three. You told him what to do, and he did it.

MRS GASCOIGNE: My word, I've never known all he did.

MINNIE: You have—everything that mattered. You maybe didn't know it was Bertha Purdy, but you knew it was some woman like her, and what did you care? *She* had the orts and slarts, you kept your son. And you want to keep him, even now. Yes—and you do keep him.

MRS GASCOIGNE: We're learnin' a thing or two, Luther.

LUTHER: Ay.

   Enter JOE.

MINNIE: Yes! What did you care about the woman who would have to take some after you? Nothing! You left her with just the slarts of a man. Yes.

MRS GASCOIGNE: Indeed! I canna see as you're so badly off. You've got a husband as doesn't drink, as waits on you hand and foot, as gives you a free hand in everything. It's you as doesn't know when you're well off, madam.

MINNIE: I'd rather have had a husband who knocked me about than a husband who was good to me because he belonged to his mother. He doesn't and can't *really* care for me. You stand before him. His *real* caring goes to *you*. Me he only wants sometimes.

JOE: She'll be in in a minute.

MRS GASCOIGNE: Tha'rt the biggest fool an' jackanapes, our Joe, as iver God made.

MINNIE: If she crosses that doorstep, then I go for good.

MRS GASCOIGNE (*bursting into fury—to* JOE): *Tha see what* thy bobby interferin' has done.

JOE: Nay—that's how it stood.

MRS GASCOIGNE: Tha mun go an' stop her, our Luther. Tell 'er it wor our Joe's foolery. An' look sharp.

LUTHER: What should *I* go for?

   LUTHER *goes out, furious.*

MINNIE: You see—you see! His mother's word is law to him. He'd do what I told him, but his *feel* would be for you. He's got no *feeling* for me. You keep all that.

MRS GASCOIGNE: You talk like a jealous woman.

MINNIE: I do! And for that matter, why doesn't Joe marry, either? Because you keep him too. You know, in spite of his bluster, he cares more for your little finger than he does for all the women in the world—or ever will. And it's wrong—it's wrong. How is a woman ever to have a husband, when the men all belong to their mothers? It's wrong.

MRS GASCOIGNE: Oh, indeed!—is it? You know, don't you? You know everything.

MINNIE: I know this, because I've suffered from it. Your elder sons you let go, and they *are* husbands. But your young sons you've kept. And Luther is your son, and the man that lives with me. But first, he's your son. And Joe ought never to marry, for he'd break a woman's heart.

MRS GASCOIGNE: Tha hears, lad! We're bein' told off.

JOE: Ah, I hear. An' what's more, it's true, Mother.

MINNIE: It is—it is. He only likes playing round me and getting some pleasure out of teasing me, because he knows I'm safely married to Luther, and can never look to him to marry me and belong to me. He's safe, so he likes me. If I were single, he'd be frightened to death of me.

JOE: Happen I should.

MRS GASCOIGNE: Tha'rt a fool.

MINNIE: And that's what you've done to me—that's my life spoiled—spoiled—ay, worse than if I'd had a drunken husband that knocked me about. For it's dead.

MRS GASCOIGNE: Tha'rt shoutin' because nowt ails thee—that's what tha art.

JOE: Nay, Mother, tha knows it's right. Tha knows tha's got me—an'll ha'e me till ter dies—an' after that—yi.

MRS GASCOIGNE: Tha talks like a fool.

JOE: And sometimes, Mother, I wish I wor dead, I do.

MINNIE: You see, you see! You see what you've done to them. It's strong women like you, who were too much for their husbands—ah!

JOE: Tha knows I couldna leave thee, Mother—tha knows I couldna. An' me, a young man, belong to thy owd age. An' there's nowheer for me to go, Mother. For tha'rt gettin' nearer to death an' yet I canna leave thee to go my own road. An' I wish, yi, often, as I wor dead.

MRS GASCOIGNE: Dunna, lad—dunna let 'er put these ideas i' thy head.

JOE: An' I can but fritter my days away. There's no goin' forrard for me.

MRS GASCOIGNE: Nay, lad, nay—what lad's better off than thee, dost reckon?

JOE: If I went t'r Australia, th' best part on me wouldna go wi' me.

MRS GASCOIGNE: Tha wunna go t'r Australia!

JOE: If I went, I should be a husk of a man. I'm allers a husk of a man, Mother. There's nowt solid about me. The' isna.

MRS GASCOIGNE: Whativer dost mean? You've a' set on me at once.

JOE: I'm nowt, Mother, an' I count for nowt. Yi, an' I know it.

MRS GASCOIGNE: Tha does. Tha sounds as if tha counts for nowt, as a rule, doesn't ter?

JOE: There's not much of a man about me. T'other chaps is more of fools, but they more of men an' a'—an' they know it.

MRS GASCOIGNE: That's thy fault.

JOE: Yi—an' will be—ter th' end o' th' chapter.

Enter LUTHER.

MINNIE: Did you tell her?

LUTHER: Yes.

MINNIE: We'll have some tea, should we?

JOE: Ay, let's. For it's bin dry work.

She sets the kettle on.

MRS GASCOIGNE: I mun be goin'.

MINNIE: Wait and have a cup of tea. I brought a cake.

JOE: But we non goin' ter ha'e it, are we, Luther, these 'ere blacklegs goin' down interferin'.

LUTHER: We arena.

MRS GASCOIGNE: But how are you going to stop them?

JOE: We s'll manage it, one road or t'other.

MRS GASCOIGNE: You'll non go gettin' yourselves into trouble.

LUTHER: We in trouble enow.

MINNIE: If you'd have had Lizzie Charley in, what should you have paid her with?

LUTHER: We should ha' found the money somewhere.

MINNIE: Do you know what I had to keep house on this week, Mother?

MRS GASCOIGNE: Not much, sin' there wor nowt but ten shillin' strike pay.

MINNIE: He gave me five shillings.

LUTHER: Tha could ha' had what things ter wanted on strap.

MINNIE: No—but why should you keep, to drink on, as much as you give me to keep house on? Five shillings!

JOE: Five bob's non a whackin' sight o' pocket money for a man's week.

MINNIE: It is, if he earns nothing. It was that as finished me off.

JOE: Well, *tha* niver ned go short—tha can let *him*.

MINNIE: I knew that was what *he* thought. But if he wouldna have my money for one thing, he wasn't going to for another.

MRS GASCOIGNE: Why, what wouldn't he have it for?

MINNIE: He wouldn't have that forty pounds, when I went on my knees to beg and beseech him to.

LUTHER: Tha did! Tha throwed it at me as if I wor a beggar as stank.

MINNIE: And you wouldn't have it when I asked you.

LUTHER: No—an' wouldna ha'e it now.

MINNIE: You can't.

LUTHER: I dunna want it.

MINNIE: And if you don't find money to keep the house on, we shall both of us starve. For you've got to keep me. And

I've got no money of my own now.

LUTHER: Why, what dost mean?

MINNIE: I mean what I say.

MRS GASCOIGNE: Why, what?

MINNIE: I was sick of having it between us. It was but a hundred and twenty. So I went to Manchester and spent it.

MRS GASCOIGNE: Tha's bin an' spent a hundred and twenty pound i' four days?

MINNIE: Yes, I have.

MRS GASCOIGNE: Whativer are we comin' to!

JOE: That wor a stroke worth two. Tell us what tha bought.

MINNIE: I bought myself a ring, for one thing. I thought if I ever had any children, and they asked me where was my engagement ring, I should have to show them something, for their father's sake. Do you like it? (*Holds out her hand to* JOE.)

JOE: My word, but that's a bobby-dazzler. Look, Mother.

MRS GASCOIGNE: H'm.

      JOE *takes the ring off.*

JOE: My word, but that's a diamond, if you like. How much did it cost?

MINNIE: Thirty pounds. I've got the bill in my pocket.

MRS GASCOIGNE: I only hope you'll niver come to want some day.

MINNIE: Luther must see to that.

JOE: And what else did ter buy?

MINNIE: I'll show you. (*Gets her bag, unlocks it, takes out three prints.*)

JOE I dunno reckon much ter these.

MRS GASCOIGNE: Nor me neither. An' how much has ter gen for them apiece?

MINNIE: That was twenty-five pounds. They're beautiful prints.

MRS GASCOIGNE: I dunna believe a word tha says.

MINNIE: I'll show you the bill. My master's a collector, and he picked them for me. He says they're well worth the money. And I like them.

MRS GASCOIGNE: Well, I niver seed such a job in my life. T-t-t-t! Well, a' I can say is, I hope tha'll niver come ter want. Throwin' good money i' th' gutter like this. Nay, I feel fair bad. Nay! T-t-t-t! Such tricks! And such bits o' dirty paper!

JOE: I'd rather ha'e the Co-op almanack.

MRS GASCOIGNE: So would I, any day! What dost say to't, our Luther?

LUTHER: 'Er does as 'er likes.

MINNIE: I had a lovely time with Mr Westlake, choosing them at the dealer's. He *is* clever.

MRS GASCOIGNE: Tha towd him tha wanted to get rid o' thy money, did ter?

MINNIE: No—I said I wanted some pictures for the parlour. and asked him if he'd help me choose.

MRS GASCOIGNE: Good money thrown away. Maybe the very bread of your children.

MINNIE: Nay, that's Luther's duty to provide.

MRS GASCOIGNE: Well, a' I can say is, I hope you may never come ter want. If our Luther died . . .

MINNIE: I should go back to work.

MRS GASCOIGNE: But what if tha'd three or four children?

MINNIE: A hundred and twenty pounds wouldn't make much odds then.

MRS GASCOIGNE: Well, a' I can say, I hope tha'lt niver live ter rue the day.

JOE: What dost think on 'er, Luther?

LUTHER: Nay, she's done as she liked with her own.

MINNIE (*emptying her purse in her lap*): I've got just seventeen shillings. You drew your strike pay yesterday. How much have you got of that, Luther?

LUTHER: Three bob.

MINNIE: And do you want to keep it?

LUTHER: Ah.

MINNIE: Very well . . . I shall spend this seventeen shillings till it's gone, and then we shall have to live on soup-tickets.

MRS GASCOIGNE: I'll back my life!

JOE: And who'll fetch the soup?

MINNIE: Oh, I shall. I've been thinking, that big jug will do nicely. I'm in the same boat as other men's wives now, and so I must do the same.

JOE: They'll gi'e you strap at West's.

MINNIE: I'm not going to run up bills, no, I'm not. I'll go to the free teas, and fetch soup, an' with ten shillings a week we shall manage.

MRS GASCOIGNE: Well, that's one road, lass.

MINNIE: It's the only one. And now, if he can provide, he must, and if he can't, he must tell me so, and I'll go back into service, and not be a burden to him.

MRS GASCOIGNE: High and mighty, high and mighty! We'll see, my lass; we'll see.

MINNIE: That's all we can do.

MRS GASCOIGNE: Tha doesna care how he takes it.

MINNIE: The prints belong to both of us. (*Hands them to* LUTHER.) You haven't said if you like them yet.

LUTHER (*taking them, suddenly rams them in the fire*): Tha can go to hell.

MINNIE (*with a cry*): Ah!—that's my ninety pounds gone. (*Tries to snatch them out.*)

MRS GASCOIGNE (*beginning to cry*): Come, Joe, let's go; let's go, my lad. I've seen as much this day as ever my eyes want to see. Let's go, my lad. (*Gets up, beginning to tie on her bonnet.*)

MINNIE (*white and intense, to* LUTHER): Should you like to throw my ring after them? It's all I've got left. (*She holds out her hand—he flings it from him.*)

LUTHER: Yi, what do I care what I do! (*Clenching his fists as if he would strike her*.)—what do I!—what do I!——

MRS GASCOIGNE (*putting on her shawl*): A day's work—a day's work! Ninety pound! Nay—nay, oh nay—nay, oh nay—nay! Let's goe, Joe, my lad. Eh, our Luther, our, Luther! Let's go, Joe. Come.

JOE: Ah, I'll come, Mother.

MRS GASCOIGNE: Luther!

LUTHER: What?

MRS GASCOIGNE: It's a day's work, it is, wi' thee. Eh dear! Come, let's go, Joe. Let's go whoam.

LUTHER: An' I'll go.

MRS GASCOIGNE: Dunna thee do nowt as ter'll repent of, Luther—dunna thee. It's thy mother axes thee. Come, Joe.

   MRS GASCOIGNE *goes out, followed by* JOE. LUTHER *stands with face averted from his wife; mutters something, reaches for his cap, goes out.* MINNIE *stands with her hand on the mantelpiece.*

CURTAIN

ACT FOUR

The following morning—about 5 a.m. A candle is burning.

MINNIE sits by the fire in a dressing-gown. She is weeping. A knock, and MRS GASCOIGNE'S voice, MINNIE goes to open the door; re-enters with her mother-in-law, the latter with a big brown shawl over her head.

MRS GASCOIGNE: Is Luther a-whoam?

MINNIE: No—he's not been in all night.

MRS GASCOIGNE: T-t-t-t! Now whereiver can they be? Joe's not in neither.

MINNIE: Isn't he?

MRS GASCOIGNE: No. He said he might be late, so I went to bed, and slept a bit uneasy-like till about four o'clock. Then I wakes up a' of a sudden, an' says: 'I'm by mysen i' th' house!' It gave me such a turn I daresn't shout. So I gets me up an' goes ter his room, an' he'd niver bin i' bed a' night. Well, I went down, but no signs nowhere. An' 'im wi' a broken arm. An' I listened an' I listened—an' then methinks I heered a gun go off. I felt as if I should die if I stopped by mysen another minute. So I on's wi' my shawl an' nips down here. There's not a soul astir nowhere. I a'most dropped when I seed your light. Hasn't Luther bin in a' night, dost say?

MINNIE: He went out with you, and he never came in again. I went to bed, thinking perhaps he'd be sleeping on the sofa. And then I came down, and he wasn't here.

MRS GASCOIGNE: Well, I've seen nowt of him, for he never come up to our house.—Now I wonder what's afoot wi' th' silly fools?

MINNIE: I thought he'd gone and left me.

MRS GASCOIGNE: It's more like some o' this strike work. When I heered that gun, I said: 'Theer goes one o' my lads!'

MINNIE: You don't think they're killed?

MRS GASCOIGNE: Heaven knows what they are. But I niver thought he'd ha' served me this trick—left me by myself without telling me, and gone cutting off a' th' night through—an' him wi' a broken arm.

MINNIE: Where do you think they've gone?

MRS GASCOIGNE: The Lord above alone knows—but I'se warrant it's one o' these riotin' tricks—stopping them blacklegs as wor goin' down to see to th' roads.

MINNIE: Do you think——?

MRS GASCOIGNE: I'll back anything. For I heered th' winding engines plain as anything. Hark!

They listen.

MINNIE: I believe I can hear them.

MRS GASCOIGNE: Th' ingines?

MINNIE: Yes.

MRS GASCOIGNE: They're winding something down. Eh dear, what a dead world it seems, wi' none o' th' pits chuffin' an' no steam wavin' by day, an' no lights shinin' by night. You may back your life there was a gang of 'em going to stop that lot of blacklegs. And there'd be soldiers for a certainty. If I didn't hear a shot, I heered summat much like one.

MINNIE: But they'd never shoot, would they?

MRS GASCOIGNE: Haven't they shot men up an' down th' country? Didn't I know them lads was pining to go an' be shot at? I did. Methinks when I heard that gun, 'They'd niver rest till this had happened.'

MINNIE: But they're not shot, Mother. You exaggerate.

MRS GASCOIGNE: I niver said they wor. But if anything happens to a man, my lass, you may back your life, nine cases out o' ten, it's a spit on th' women.

MINNIE: Oh, what a thing to say! Why, there are accidents.

MRS GASCOIGNE: Yes, an' men verily gets accidents, to pay us out, I do believe. They get huffed up, they bend down their faces, and they say to theirselves: 'Now I'll get myself hurt, an' she'll be sorry,' else: 'Now I'll get myself killed, an' she'll ha'e nobody to sleep wi' 'er, an's nobody to nag at.' Oh, my lass, I've had a husband an' six sons. Children they are, these men, but, my word, they're revengeful children. Children men is a' the days o' their lives. But they're master of us women when their dander's up, an' they pay us back double an' treble—they do—an' you mun allers expect it.

MINNIE: But if they went to stop the blacklegs, they wouldn't be doing it to spite us.

MRS GASCOIGNE: Wouldn't they! Yi, but they would. My lads 'ud do it to spite me, an' our Luther 'ud do it to spite thee. Yes—and it's trew. For they'd run theirselves into danger and lick their lips for joy, thinking, if I'm killed, then *she* maun lay me out. Yi—I seed it in our mester. He got killed a' pit. An' when I laid him out, his face wor that grim, an' his body that stiff, an' it said as plain as plain: 'Nowthen, you've done for me.' For it's risky work, handlin' men, my lass, an' niver thee pray for sons—— Not but what daughters is any good. Th' world is made o' men, for me, lass—there's only the men for me. An' tha'rt similar. An' so, tha'lt reap trouble by the peck, an' sorrow by the bushel. For when a woman builds her life on men, either husbands or sons, she builds on summat as sooner or later brings the house down crash on her head—yi, she does.

MINNIE: But it depends how and what she builds.

MRS GASCOIGNE: It depends, it depends. An' tha thinks tha can steer clear o' what I've done. An' perhaps tha can. But steer clear the whole length o' th' road, tha canna, an' tha'lt see. Nay, a childt is a troublesome pleasure to a woman, but a man's a trouble pure and simple.

MINNIE: I'm sure it depends what you make of him.

MRS GASCOIGNE: Maybe—maybe. But I've allers tried to do my best, i' spite o' what tha said against me this afternoon.

MINNIE: I didn't mean it—I was in a rage.

MRS GASCOIGNE: Yi, tha meant it plain enow. But I've tried an' tried my best for my lads, I have—an' this is what owd age brings me—wi' 'em.

MINNIE: Nay, Mother—nay. See how fond they are of you.

MRS GASCOIGNE: Yi—an' they go now i' their mischief, yes, tryin' to get killed, to spite me. Yi!

MINNIE: Nay. Nay.

MRS GASCOIGNE: It's true. An' tha can ha'e Luther. Tha'lt get him, an' tha can ha'e him.

MINNIE: Do you think I shall?

MRS GASCOIGNE: I can see. Tha'lt get him—but tha'lt get sorrow wi' 'em, an' wi' th' sons tha has. See if tha doesna.

MINNIE: But I don't care. Only don't keep him from me. It leaves me so—with nothing—not even trouble.

MRS GASCOIGNE: He'll come to thee—an' he'll think no more o' me as his mother than he will o' that poker.

MINNIE: Oh, no—oh, no.

MRS GASCOIGNE: Yi—I know well—an' then that other.

There is a silence—the two women listening.

MINNIE: If they'd been hurt, we should ha' known by now.

MRS GASCOIGNE: Happen we should. If they come, they'll come together. An' they'll come to this house first.

A silence. MINNIE *starts.*

Did ter hear owt?

MINNIE: Somebody got over the stile.

MRS GASCOIGNE (*listening*): Yi.

MINNIE (*listening*): It *is* somebody.

MRS GASCOIGNE: I' t'street.

MINNIE (*starting up*): Yes.

MRS GASCOIGNE: Comin'? It's Luther. (*Goes to the door.*)

An' it's on'y Luther.

Both women stand, the mother nearer the door. The door opens—a slight sluther. Enter LUTHER, *with blood on his face—rather shaky and dishevelled.*

My boy! my boy!

LUTHER: Mother! (*He goes blindly.*) Where's Minnie?

MINNIE (*with a cry*): Oh!

MRS GASCOIGNE: Wheer's Joe?—wheer's our Joe?

LUTHER (*to* MINNIE, *queer, stunned, almost polite*): It worn't 'cause I wor mad wi' thee I didna come whoam.

MRS GASCOIGNE (*clutching him sternly*): Where's Joe?

LUTHER: He's gone up street—he thought tha might ha' wakkened.

MRS GASCOIGNE: Wakkened enow.

MRS GASCOIGNE *goes out.*

MINNIE: Oh, what have you done?

LUTHER: We'd promised not to tell nobody—else I should. We stopped them blacklegs—leastways—but it worn't because I—I—— (*He stops to think.*) I wor mad wi' thee, as I didna come whoam.

MINNIE: What have you done to your head?

LUTHER: It wor a stone or summat catched it. It's gev me a headache. Tha mun—tha mun tie a rag round it—if ter will. (*He sways as he takes his cap off.*)

She catches him in her arms. He leans on her as if he were tipsy.

Minnie——

MINNIE: My love—my love!

LUTHER: Minnie—I want thee ter ma'e what tha can o' me. (*He sounds almost sleepy.*)

MINNIE (*crying*): My love—my love!

LUTHER: I know what tha says is true.

MINNIE: No, my love—it isn't—it isn't.

LUTHER: But if ter'lt ma'e what ter can o' me—an' then if ter has a childt—tha'lt happen ha'e enow.

MINNIE: No—no—it's you. It's you I want. It's you.

LUTHER: But tha's allers had me.

MINNIE: No, never—and it hurt so.

LUTHER: I thowt tha despised me.

MINNIE: Ah—my love!

LUTHER: Dunna say I'm mean, to me—an' got no go.

MINNIE: I only said it because you wouldn't let me love you.

LUTHER: Tha didna love me.

MINNIE: Ha!—it was *you*.

LUTHER: Yi. (*He looses himself and sits down heavily.*) I'll ta'e my boots off. (*He bends forward.*)

MINNIE: Let me do them. (*He sits up again.*)

LUTHER: It's started bleedin'. I'll do 'em i' ha'cf a minute.

MINNIE: No—trust me—trust yourself to me. Let me have you now for my own. (*She begins to undo his boots.*)

LUTHER: Dost want me?

MINNIE (*she kisses his hands*): Oh, my love! (*She takes him in her arms.*)

   He suddenly begins to cry.

CURTAIN

AFTER READING THE PLAY:
THE WIDOWING OF MRS HOLROYD

Keeping Track

Act One, Scene 1

1 Where is Charles Holroyd when the play opens?
2 Mrs Holroyd says that her husband has 'disgraced' her before this most recent incident. How?
3 Why do the Holroyd's live outside Bestwood—in a lonely cottage near to the pit?
4 Mrs Holroyd says, 'There's less than nothing if you can't be like the rest of them.' What does she mean?
5 Why are the children, Jack and Minnie, afraid of their father?
6 Why is Blackmore at the Holroyd cottage? Find evidence to support your answer.

Act One, Scene 2

1 Describe Clara and Laura.
2 Why have they come to the Holroyd home?
3 There has been a good deal to suggest, so far in the play, that Mrs Holroyd is dissatisfied with her husband. What evidence can you find in this scene to suggest that *he* resents her? How significant is the way the two speak?
4 Given the Holroyd's mutual dissatisfaction with the marriage, what evidence can you find in this scene to explain why they married, and why they remain together?

Act Two

1 Can you suggest why Blackmore brings Holroyd home?
2 Holroyd says, 'It's him tha cuts tha cloth by, is it?' What does this mean?
3 Why does Holroyd attack Blackmore? How does Blackmore respond? (At one point Blackmore says, 'Mind what tha'rt doing'—do you see any significance in this alteration in the way Blackmore normally speaks?)
4 Summarise Mrs Holroyd's account of how she came to marry her husband. Why, according to her, has the marriage failed?

5 What is Blackmore's proposed solution to the problem? How does Mrs Holroyd respond to this suggestion?

Act Three

1 How does Holroyd's mother (the Grandmother) justify his drinking?
2 What does the Grandmother identify as the real problem with the marriage? How does she say the Bestwood community sees Mrs Holroyd?
3 Why is the miner, Rigley, uneasy about Holroyd's whereabouts?
4 How has Holroyd been killed? Is the manner of his death particularly significant given the nature of his unhappiness when alive?
5 Why does Mrs Holroyd feel guilty?
6 Do you think the relationship between Mrs Holroyd and Blackmore will continue after the end of the play? Give evidence in support of your answer.
7 Do you see any significance in the Grandmother's mention of her husband's response to their son's death?
8 Try to describe the exact nature of the two women's grief as they wash the body.
9 What do you think D. H. Lawrence would want Mrs Holroyd to do after the events of the play:
      a. Marry Blackmore? (Given that he is more sensitive and caring than Holroyd was.)
      b. Not marry at all?
Give reasons for your answer.

Explorations

1 Write (or improvise) a scene in which Charles Holroyd meets Clara some time after the incident when he took Clara and Laura to his home. He had told them, on that occasion, that he did not have a wife—and the two women had gone along to test the truth of his assertion. In this new scene Clara tries to find out from Holroyd *why* he misled her.
2 Write the story of Charles Holroyd's funeral. Concentrate upon

the thoughts (and memories) of Lizzie Holroyd and Charles Holroyd's mother.

3 After the funeral Blackmore writes a letter to Lizzie in which he tries to convince her that she should come away with him. Lizzie replies—telling him what she will do. Write both these letters.

Special Studies

1 *The Inquest*

Write a short (one act) play which describes the inquest on Charles Holroyd. The Coroner will want to know how Holroyd died and why. Beginning, perhaps, with Rigley (the last person to see Holroyd alive) he will call all the characters of the play to question them on Holroyd's character, his state of mind at the time of his death and the reasons for his apparent unhappiness on the day he died. As well as each character making a statement about how they saw the situation, the Coroner might ask questions. At the end he will make a judgement about the cause of death (accident, suicide, negligence of the mining company).

2 *The Widowing of Mrs Holroyd and Odour of Chrysanthemums*

When you have found and read Lawrence's short story, *Odour of Chrysanthemums*, you will see immediately that it is very similar to *The Widowing of Mrs Holroyd*. Compare, in essay form these two pieces by D. H. Lawrence. Look particularly at the following elements:

- *a.* the resentment the husbands and wives feel towards each other, and why they feel as they do;
- *b.* the final scene of the play, and the final scene of the story. How does the wife feel? What view of her husband and their life together does she have?
- *c.* The story was written in 1909 and revised in 1911; the play was written in 1910 and revised in 1913. Lawrence was probably experimenting with *form* using essentially the same ideas. Which of the two do you find more powerful? Give reasons for your answer.

AFTER READING THE PLAY:
THE DAUGHTER-IN-LAW

Keeping Track

Act One, Scene 1

1 Exactly how did Joe break his arm? What does this tell you about the sort of person he is?

2 What happened when Joe tried to claim 'accident pay'? How did he go about trying to deceive his employers? What do his attempts at deception tell you about him?

3 How does his mother, Mrs Gascoigne, respond to these reported events?

4 Find and write down a quotation which you think expresses Joe's view of the company he works for.

5 What are Mrs Gascoigne's views on marriage?

6 What does Mrs Gascoigne mean by the following:
    a. 'Why, wheer's th' loaf as tha'd like to gnawg a' thy life?'
    b. 'Tha's done thysen harm enow for one day, wi' thy tongue.'
    c. 'An' swilled thy belly afore that, methinks.'

7 What does Mrs Gascoigne think about strikes?

8 What does Mrs Purdy say about the mining company? What is her view of the impending strike?

9 Why has Mrs Purdy come to the Gascoigne house?

10 How did Luther come to go out with Bertha Purdy?

11 What does Mrs Purdy say about the fate of women in their community?

12 How did Luther come to marry Minnie? What picture of Minnie do you get from Mrs Gascoigne's description? What impression do you get of Luther?

13 What point is Joe making when he says, 'If ever I get married, Mother, I s'll go i' lodgin's six month aforehand.'?

14 What is Mrs Gascoigne's advice to Mrs Purdy?

15 Does Joe agree with his mother's advice? What does he say?

138

Act One, Scene 2

1 Apart from her age, we should notice an immediate difference between Minnie and the two women presented in the first scene. What is that difference?

2 Minnie says to Luther, 'Oh, you *are* a nuisance!' In what ways does she see him as 'such a bother'?

3 Luther asks Minnie if she's 'been up home'. Do you see any significance in this short section of the scene—where visiting Mrs Gascoigne is discussed?

4 Why is Minnie fascinated by Luther's mouth as he eats. How is this part of the scene a contrast to what has gone before?

5 What is it that starts an argument between Luther and Minnie?

6 What does Minnie say about the possible strike? Look back at the points Mrs Gascoigne and Mrs Purdy made about strikes, (Questions 6 and 7 above). Are there similarities in the views of the three women?

7 What does Minnie say about Luther's mother?

8 Suggest why Joe behaves as he does immediately after arriving.

9 How does Luther take the news that Bertha is 'with childt'?

10 Mrs Purdy, and Bertha, are very different from Minnie. How?

11 How does Luther behave when Minnie and Joe return? How would you describe his mood?

12 What exactly does Minnie mean when she says to Joe (after Luther has left), 'You don't know how hard it is, with a man as—as leaves you alone all the time.'?

Act Two

1 What is Luther's mood at the beginning of Act Two?

2 We have already seen Luther and Minnie arguing (in Act One, Scene 2). Exactly how is this row different?

3 Can you find any evidence to suggest that Minnie is surprised by Luther's responses during the early part of this scene?

4 What does Minnie mean by the word 'coward'?

5 Minnie uses the word 'mean' of Luther. How is he 'mean' in her eyes?

6 Does she *want* to leave him? Give evidence in support of your answer.

7 What do you think is the most hurtful thing Minnie says to Luther during this scene?

8 Who does Minnie blame for this situation? Write down what she says.
9 Imagine you were giving advice to an actress playing the part of Minnie. Identify for the actress the main stages of the scene, Minnie's state of mind and her feelings as the scene progresses.
10 Try the same for Luther.

Act Three
1 Where has Minnie been, and for how long?
2 What has been happening in her absence?
3 How is the strike compared with the difficulties between Luther and Minnie?
4 Summarise Minnie's views on Mrs Gascoigne and her part in 'what ails' the marriage between Minnie and Luther.
5 How does Mrs Gascoigne defend herself? Summarise her arguments.
6 What has Minnie done with her money? Why do you think she has acted in this way?
7 How does Luther react to Minnie's actions?

Act Four
1 Why does Mrs Gascoigne come to Minnie?
2 What does Mrs Gascoigne say about men?
3 What happens in the last scene—between Luther and Minnie?
4 The whole play might be seen as a series of battles. Who have the battles been between? Which battle do you think is the main one?

Explorations

1 Write (or improvise) a scene between Luther and Bertha in which he talks to her about the baby she is expecting and his relationship with Minnie.
2 Write a scene between Minnie and Mr Westlake (her former employer) in which she tells him about the troubles she is having in her marriage.
3 Write a newspaper feature called, 'Miner's Wives'. You might include interviews with Mrs Gascoigne, Mrs Purdy and Minnie as part of the article.
4 Put together a newspaper front page about the miner's strike

described in the play. Perhaps the arrival of the army to help might be the occasion of the headline, interviews, exclusives and latest news. Include all the material you would expect to see on the front page of a local newspaper—advertisements, stop press, stories inside etc. The date would be 1912 (possibly February) and the newspaper might be called the 'Eastwood Echo'.

Special Studies

1 *Two interviews*
Imagine you have been asked to help Minnie and Luther patch up their differences. Interview each of them separately—in order to clarify exactly what the differences are between them. Make sure you have them list all their grievances.

Conclude the two interviews by getting them both together and pointing out to them the reasons, as you see them, for their constant battling, and suggest to them how they might make things easier for themselves.

2 *'The Daughter-in-Law' as a series of battles*
Describe the various battles which take place in the play:
—between miners and mine owners;
—between mother and sons;
—between wife and husband.
Are these battles resolved by the end of the play? Which do you think Lawrence treats as central to the play?

3 *'The Daughter-in-Law' and 'Fanny and Annie'*
Find and read *Fanny and Annie* (written by Lawrence in 1919). Discuss the similarities of situation and theme, (has Lawrence clarified his main concern in this later story?). Look particularly at how Fanny is faced with a choice between the gentle and the passionate (between middle class and working class, between social respectability and the erotic feeling she has towards Harry and which she recognises in herself). Compare this with the way Minnie feels towards Luther. Act One Scene 2, and the last scene of the play need looking at closely.

Put all this together in the form of an essay.

Looking at the two plays together

1 An imagined interview with D. H. Lawrence

There are many questions which you should be able to invent
concerning Lawrence's main intentions in these two plays. Among
them you might like to include questions aimed to discover
Lawrence's views on: marriage, mothers and sons, the working
class in general and working class women in particular.

2 Recurring themes and situations in some of the plays and stories of D. H. Lawrence

You may have already looked at *Odour of Chrysanthemums* and
Fanny and Annie in the 'Special Studies' section of these suggestions
for coursework. There are other stories which contain similar
situations and themes to those dealt with in the plays, and it would
make an interesting piece of extended coursework to look at these
in relation to the plays. Apart from those already mentioned see:
Her Turn; *Strike Pay*; *The Miner at Home* and *A Sick Collier*. See also
the poem, *The Collier's Wife*, and for those who find themselves
developing an enthusiasm for Lawrence's work, look at the novel,
Sons and Lovers.

You will find it interesting to discover how often Lawrence
returned to similar themes and situations again and again in his
early work.

3 The social background to the plays

Using the two plays as source material, put together an extended
study (in the form of an essay, or a documentary with interviews
etc) about the society in which the two plays take place. What do
the plays tell you about: the conditions of work for miners; strikes;
the living conditions of miners' families; the nature of mining
communities; the place of women in these communities; social
problems (poverty and drink, for instance)? You might also consider how much you think conditions have changed in working
class communities since the time of the plays.